Stages of LIFE

DOUG POOLE

WESTBOW
PRESS®
A DIVISION OF THOMAS NELSON
& ZONDERVAN

WestBow Press books may be ordered through booksellers or by contacting:

WestBow Press
A Division of Thomas Nelson & Zondervan
1663 Liberty Drive
Bloomington, IN 47403
www.westbowpress.com
844-714-3454

ISBN: 978-1-6642-2896-2 (sc)
ISBN: 978-1-6642-2897-9 (hc)
ISBN: 978-1-6642-2895-5 (e)

Library of Congress Control Number: 2021906186

Print information available on the last page.

WestBow Press rev. date: 5/18/2021

Contents

Preface

Becoming an Author — God's Way

Calling yourself an author can be a bit humbling when you know deep down inside you don't possess the talent to write very well and then put your name on a book cover.

In yielding to the writing of a book, I found many excuses to let it slide by because I did not know how. It was a task taking more skills than I possessed. It was difficult to imagine what all was needed to start and accomplish such a task.

The writing of my first book, Coming Before the LORD, was quite an ordeal for me as I wrestled with my feelings, emotions, thoughts and reluctance to begin then follow through. As time passed I would write short excerpts as they came to mind and kept them saved in a stack of papers in my study.

The stack kept getting bigger and I thought it was becoming continually more difficult to organize the pile of ideas and Scriptures the Lord was placing in my mind. Where do I find help to sort it out and assimilate a book?

Sometimes I would think I needed to gather up the separate notes and determine if I really had enough to write a book. Maybe there wasn't enough information for a whole book? Once I considered the possibility, I did not see that happening as I pondered how to do it. The unknown caused me to doubt myself, so I would quit trying.

One day I realized the Lord was insisting on me writing a book and the impressions and Scriptures He was bringing my way could provide the information needed to answer His calling on my life. Even late in life did not matter. Then, I thought maybe I had waited too long, but no — the prompting continued.

So, I sat down one day and tried to lay out the many papers I had written and the task seemed too much for me to handle. I would get overwhelmed with the volume of information and although I was good at organizing it — still, a book seemed too much to tackle.

After I decided to do the best I could in organizing the gathered information, I found myself looking at ten separate stacks with some continuity and sense to it all. The ten stacks became my book chapters, and so my new journey began.

I had such an urgency to write, it became almost an emergency within me, and I felt that I had to learn someway to accomplish this endeavor and follow my continued promptings from the Lord. It was like being pushed downhill, and the further I went, the faster I began to move forward.

I felt the Lord was telling me that talent wasn't what I needed. All He wanted was a willing vessel. So the problem wasn't my lack of ability after all — it was my unwillingness to follow His leading!

After reading Scripture one day, I realized if God was prompting me, I had better step out in faith and see if this book could become a reality. What would it hurt since if it didn't come together — I could at least say I tried?

Sure enough — that step of faith caused me to get excited inside even more, and my spirit began to rise to a new level of activity. It rose to such a level I could not bail out and remain normal or settled in my spirit if I ignored His promptings.

Normal was never my strong suit, either. I discovered it really was the Lord prompting me, and He was waiting for me to get with it. My normalcy can be summed up like a friend of mine tells me: 'It's not that I'm wrong, but there is something about me that's just not right.'

Scripture does say that we believers are a peculiar people, and I found biblical confirmation for this in Titus 2:14 and 1 Peter 2:9 in the King James Version of the bible. I had always thought before that I was a little different — only a little. My difference amounted to my sense of humor. Anyway, it hasn't been too earth-shaking to now be called 'peculiar' since the bible says every believer is peculiar — somewhat like me.

As I said, the sorted-out piles of notes became the chapters for my first book. When it was completed, I found relief and determined that I could finally return to normal. Nope — I discovered my new normal was now different. This experience had given me insight into the bible I did not know existed. It gave me a confidence that I could do it.

Because of my lack of writing abilities and many excuses, I took a total of 12 years to finish the first manuscript. It always seemed there were obstacles everywhere — waiting constantly for a good reason to excuse my progress. It became a habit to avoid completing because I would get started then become overwhelmed and stop. At the time, I was trying to care for my sick wife, and that was always a good excuse.

But finally, I completed all that's necessary to send off the manuscript, and the end was in sight. A sense of relief was welling up inside of me because my attention was on the fact my book would finally be complete, and I wouldn't have something inside telling me to finish.

And, just when I finished it and sent the manuscript off to a publisher, I though that was the end to this new adventure, and I would once again become settled on the inside. I would finally be relieved of any guilt for finding excuses to never complete the project.

Such was not the case. The Lord then gave me a second book to write. I was so surprised I waited a week before starting to make sure it wasn't just excitement from finally completing the first project I had worked so hard to finish. Then, after that one week I started on the second book, Remember the WORD, and it came quickly. Once I had written down several life lessons learned, I discovered the makings for my second book, and each chapter's title. After eight months, it too was sent off to the publishers.

The Lord had provided mental pictures for both book covers that were brought to life by each separate publisher, and they instantly were confirmed in my spirit. The publisher's Cover Design

Department each produced exactly what I saw in the mental pictures that I believed the Lord had presented in my mind.

Then, when I was dealing with the many details that are required to complete publishing a book and get it on the market, He gave me a third book to write! This time I was more eager because I had learned enough to somewhat know what I was doing.

Looking back, I remember telling Him I was giving in to whatever He wanted me to do since I was now retired. In yielding my will to Him during prayer, I put myself out there once again, thinking it was all over, and life would slow down. Little did I know that more was on the way during that prayer, and a willing vessel was what I needed to be once again.

As I now view the circumstances, I think He wanted to see if I was serious in what I had prayed. You know, did I really mean I was willing to do whatever He wanted me to do. Since I was serious, He immediately began to flood my mind and spirit with more information from the bible needed to start writing again. The title and cover design immediately followed, so I put it on paper using my 3rd grade art talent, and book number three was born.

I was more eager to listen this time because I had learned so much doing the first two books. I didn't want to fall behind and have to struggle to put it all together like before. Hopefully, what I had learned up to this point would help me stay on target and expedite all required to put the third book together.

As I said, the cover design for the third book came quickly, but the subject matter was a bit foreign to my thinking, and I needed a great deal from the Lord to compile and understand what it all meant. I had many holes in my thinking that would soon be filled as I read the Word and prayed for answers.

He provided me with a mental picture of what He wanted, and when I put it on paper, a diagram evolved. This diagram was so detailed it revealed exactly what the book was to include with a swarm of biblical references, and how to put it all together in sequence all came to mind.

The diagram provided me an outline to follow and included the different aspects we can each experience in life. The progression of levels, the different phases and seasons are common issues we all face as we travel through life. The clarification for this book came into focus with understanding as I started to put it in writing.

The Diagram

This book's writing came to me by impressions, dreams, and an urgency I felt from the Lord's continued promptings. An urgency to put in a book for others to read and learn from its contents. As I said, I had to listen carefully to write it on paper, but the joy of learning became very intriguing to me as I prayed and studied in gathering biblical support.

The first impression I received was that diagram of what the Stages of Life consisted of and some biblical references to support the meaning and application. I needed an outline from which to start writing, and this diagram provided what I needed to begin.

The diagram is presented on the back cover of this book and in Appendix I. It was the visual picture given me to understand the path needed to help explain the different stages of life and how it all comes together. As you see, we are introduced at conception (Stage 1), and once born into the world (Stage 2), it reveals where humanity is brought into the world to live a life on earth.

Stage 3 is Hades or Eternal damnation. Once we are born into the world, we become a fallen human being destined to Hades because of the fall of man in the Garden of Eden (the location of the Original Sin). Compliments of Adam and Eve in utilizing their free choice privileges and being disobedient to God by choosing what they desired instead of obedience to God (Galatians 6:7, 8).

Choosing to be disobedient to God does have consequences that will be unwanted later on in life. The momentary gratification of self-pleasures will pass, but be certain negative consequences will follow when this kind of seed is sown. It may not be immediately, but be assured the results will emerge, and you will reap your justly reward.

We can pray for forgiveness for acting out the sin, but that does not necessarily erase or negate the results of our sinful choices. This choice to sin is what brought about Stage 3 and placed a destination not intended by God for humankind. Remember, God is holy and cannot cohabitant with anything evil or unholy (Habakkuk 1:13).

But, now, when we enter the world at our physical birth, we become automatically entered into sin and the consequences that will follow if not resolved. Why? Because sin has a penalty, and we are subject to its consequences just by entering the world at birth.

The good part is God sent His Son as a sacrifice to pay the results of the sin committed in the Garden of Eden so each person born into the world would have an option to Passover Stage 3 and escape sins punishment. God predetermined this option because He knew how humanity would respond before He created the human race.

The bridge over Stage 3 provides all humanity with a means to escape the consequences of Adam and Eve's sin in the Garden. But as an option, this means you can accept Christ as your Savior and proceed over sin's consequences and avoid Hades and Eternal damnation altogether. That is our option to overcome our fallen state. We can Passover this stage by faith in Christ.

The option available to find a way out from our physical birth's entry into the world and the consequences is straightforward. The option God has provided through His Son's sacrifice on the cross can resolve this issue we had no control over or anyway to avoid. Since we had no way to get out of the sin penalty, God sent His Son, Jesus, to give us an option.

We now can choose for ourselves where we want to spend eternity. This option is known as your spiritual birth — born again. Once you accept Jesus as your Savior, your spiritual birth takes place. This spiritual birth brings the Spirit of God — the Holy Spirit into your being and enlightens the limited perspective you once had (John 14: Acts 9:17; 1 John 2:20 & 27).

Your born again experience will place you in Stage 4 immediately, and begin a whole new perspective on life and give you spiritual guidance to follow and function through a entirely new set of possibilities you didn't know even existed.

Once we accept the Lord, the bible will start to come alive when you read Scripture. Your understanding will be expanded to receive more than ever imagined. What was once hard to read and difficult to understand will significantly expand, and you'll see like never thought possible? The blind once covering your spiritual vision has been lifted, and your visibility will include a new set of spiritual eyes to see all around you (John 9:35).

Stage 4 begins the life God intended for humanity in the first place. That is until the Garden couple messed it all up. As I said before, this was no surprise to God. He already had a plan to override this blunder of humanity even before the world was created. Jesus had already agreed to accept the challenge to sacrifice Himself to save fallen man (John 1:1, 4, 14; 3:34; 6:63 & 68).

God was well aware a human being with a choice had the freedom to select whatever they wanted. God granted our freedom to choose intentionally and already knew the outcome. Since God does not want robot-like people to do fellowship with (no human feelings or reactions), He selected human beings instead who can choose for themselves.

As I said, since God does not want robots to fellowship with, He selected humans, giving them the freedom to choose for themselves. I'm certain fellowship with a robot could be quite dull. But humankind — now that would bring excitement and hopefully a willing vessel to love — a person to fellowship with rather than an object. God wants a relationship — not a dictatorship!

This book, Stages of Life, also includes color where all in the past had been black and white. Color was another new experience with the Lord for me. I never thought much about color before, but I had to consider who was providing the information —right?

When this book was about 50% done, I became more excited as it became colorfully visible and with clarity and a greater understanding. It was shaping up like God had impressed upon me with details that supported what I was finding in the bible.

I now understood what He wanted, and the big picture became even more vivid to me. Seeing a more completed product caused me to be more eager to put it on paper. I did begin to visualize what it was going to look like, but I still wanted to see the final result.

As time moved forward, I ask Him if he would look over what I had written and show me how to illuminate the biblical situations and life stories that would reflect His meaning by example, more clearly. And, He did just that.

I ask Him for any direction necessary to get this book right, so it would explain what He intended to the very best of my understanding At this point, I realized again; I was only the penman, so I needed to listen very carefully.

As I sat down to try and listen to Him, the ideas started coming, and once I wrote down all that came to mind, I knew the Holy Spirit was completing in me what I needed to know. From my perspective, to have the complete message for Stages of Life was deemed critical. I wanted to be finished and with more defined details to reveal His purpose and message intended for others.

As I look back at the first and second books I'd written, I realized that my name should be written as co-author because all I did was write it down like He revealed it to me. He provided the cover design, collective messages, and all the contents, subject matter, and plenty of ideas, plus a diagram to follow. All I did was transfer it to paper.

All through this new experience as book three ran through my mind, I found myself responding to His urgent promptings and waiting for guidance. Doing so made the process much easier, and my fear of being incomplete began to fade.

I found myself intrigued with the new process and eager to experience more. As I viewed the different thoughts He was giving me, it again became crystal clear that I was only a helper. But, the idea of being a helper for the Lord was just fine with me.

If I put on the cover that the Lord and I wrote the books together, I can only imagine what folks might assume. I didn't want to sound so spiritual that I thought myself 'higher' than anyone else. Believe me; I know very well where I'm at with the Lord. Right in the middle of the cluster of believers in existence today.

I know where I'm positioned with the Lord based on Scripture. I know I have favor just like every other believer, and I like that. I'm learning and growing as fast as I can to accomplish in life what He sent me here to do. His input has caused me to relish His presence, and it gives me hope for what lies ahead.

Besides, it's not who I am, but who I am in Christ that gives me any level of acceptance in God's eyes. God sees me in Christ, and that changed everything about my position with Him. I'm a child of the King and eager to tell others what they can receive and accomplish if they follow His direction and not hesitate or procrastinate like I did.

Putting off serving the Lord limits your possibilities and lessens your actual accomplishments in life. Since we only have one life to live, we should give it all we can while there is still time. It is limited time, you know?

Now that I'm finally getting more adapted to following His leading, I will need to live for 120 years to accomplish all I now think the Lord wants me to do. I wish I had started sooner listening to the Lord; then, I wouldn't have to live quite so long!

These lessons I'm learning about yielding to the Lord will hopefully cause you to look at yourself. Maybe His calling on your life has been placed on hold, awaiting your response to His promptings. Be careful and don't wait too long. Remember, the Lord only needs a willing vessel. He takes care of all the remaining necessities required to complete a project of His doing. Why not be a conduit for the Lord and get excited in the process?

So the question that comes with all of this can be viewed quite simply — how willing are you to follow the Lord's prompting in your life? Really — how willing are you to set aside your plans and see what He has for you?

As I thought about this book's actual source, I discovered I don't know how to get the Lord to sign His name as author. So, I went ahead and put my name on the cover as author because of the mentioned difficulties. Do remember, though, I'm only the penman, and the Holy Spirit of God made me do it. That's the only excuse I have now for writing this book. Besides, my position is personal, and — That's my story and I'm sticking to it!

As I said, since I was unable to get a signature from the real book author, so I have included the following credits to emphasize my point:

Cover Design: by Divine Inspiration
Promptings of this book: by the Holy Spirit
Contents: Bible Scriptures/Principles
Relentless faithfulness: by the Lord in hot pursuit of a willing penman

All the provisions and contents are compliments of the Lord because the penman was in serious need of His help to assimilate this message and type it on paper. Relatively slow as well, I might add, but eager to comply none-the-less.

Doug Poole
Penman: Doug Poole

P.S. Maybe I should have used a 'pen' name instead of my own — you think?

Introduction

The bible has been a tremendous source for the information referenced in this book. To learn and better understand the several stages and seasons we experience in life has been an interesting subject in which to write.

The different stages accompanied by seasons with numerous variations of difficulty make up our entire life as we know it on earth. Our physical existence involves many facets that together encompass life as a whole. Looking at these areas more closely develops a better understanding of how things are and relates a way of life we each experience in common. It also reveals the possibilities God has made available for our quality of life by following His directions and applying His biblical principles.

Seeing how the different stages and variations relate to life that will occur does include our age, physical living conditions, and how life gives special meaning to each season. The receptiveness of how things operate is very interesting. Then, taking a biblical approach to explain details from a scriptural perspective and how they are applied enlightens our spectrum to understand better and visualize the whole environment in which we exist.

Living is a combination of every detail, and how the Lord uses each challenge and circumstance to grow us up and teach us principles from His vast source of wisdom is fascinating and exhilarating, to say the least. Learning His wisdom and applying it to everyday life provides benefits beyond our natural abilities and comprehension. His Word offers new understanding, which begins at our spiritual birth and starts the process of growing in the Lord and experiencing life in a whole new way, not possible without Him.

Writing this book caused me to realize how significant our circumstances can be and the predictable and unseen problems that we encounter. A closer look with direct reflection on biblical truths adjusted my personal perspective and enlarged my restricted viewpoint. Each of our lives are so different yet very similar. As I learned, I became somewhat puzzled how truths from Scripture could provide us with basic principles that could help us.

Assimilating the biblical applications available through reading God's Word became so interesting I wrote down their involvement from the diagram the Lord had placed in my mind. This concept regarding stages based on choices we make and what God has made available through the provisions Jesus made possible caused me to see a plan that was available and had been put into effect by God.

As I began to contemplate each stage, I questioned my knowledge to put on paper what was going through my mind and spirit. Our God has gifted people with ability to write and project on paper their thoughts, feelings, and what our emotions with colorful descriptive words as they rely on that gift. My realization became apparent; I did not possess that talent and I was to rely on what the Lord was showing me and not be concerned about anything else.

When I read the following Scriptures, I realized the Lord could use me, and it did not depend on my abilities, but rather on my willingness to be used by the master carpenter. This realization was a surprising revelation and released me from being self-conscious about what I could or could not do.

The Following Verses are Taken from Isaiah

Isaiah 10:14-16
"But can the ax boast greater power than the person who uses it? Is the saw greater than the person who saws? Can a rod strike unless a hand moves it? Can a wooden cane walk by itself?"

The answer is NO to all the above questions! The tool is not greater than the craftsman that is using it. I needed to realize was that if I allowed the Lord to use me, I had to believe He would help me with this transfer of information into written form — a book.

> Ephesians 3:20:
> *"Now all glory to God, who is able, through his mighty power at work within us, to accomplish infinitely more than we might ask or think."*

Could it be that God is Working in You?

> Philippians 2:13:
> *"For God is working in you, giving you the desire and the power to do what pleases him."*

His working in us is how we become His hands and feet to accomplish His Will on the earth. The key to being used by the Lord is to be willing and offer yourself a living sacrifice (Romans 12:1). Don't be so concerned how gifted you are in any particular area He directs your attention.

Sometimes we focus too much on our gifts and miss opportunities to be His 'ax,' or to be the 'saw' or to be the 'cane.' The Lord does want to use us to accomplish and carry out His work on the earth. He wants us to put our trust in Him and step out in faith. Our unique abilities, or lack of them, are not necessary to work for the Lord.

When He inspires you, I have discovered that I first, step out in faith and just do it! Then, watch with amazement, how functional you become in doing work for Him under His careful direction. I would imagine you will probably surprise yourself and learn that the Carpenter is the skilled one and what He needs is your willingness to help Him complete the job.

When I look at the books that I have written, I know who inspired them, and I know that I only wrote it down. I don't say this to sound super-spiritual, but it lets me know who made it possible using a willing vessel. My willingness was the key in starting the flow of His Holy Spirit in my life. There was not any need for special talents or gifting.

Being the penman for Him still offers the personality of the writer, but the source for the truth is still from the Lord. His principles remain scripturally factual but have a slight twist as they are processed and typed on paper through a human being.

The Lord is my source, and so I wrote down what He inspired me to put on paper. I can type, and I can hear from the Lord. In doing this, I thoroughly enjoy the process as long as I focused on the Lord. I have tried to write by myself but quickly learn the difference and start over again, keeping my eyes and ears open to His still small voice. My lack of talent was superseded by His power working in me and provides an opportunity never before even thought possible.

My action in faith started me being apart of His doing, which is beyond my scope of understanding, and I'm okay with that. I will learn more about how He is using me in the near future, and I'm sure I will get even more excited.

I consider it blind faith, but faith is what pleases Him, so I believe that I get to go along for the ride, so I had better learn how to enjoy the journey (Hebrews 11:6). This way, we're both happy, and the penman gets in on a portion of what God is doing.

CHAPTER ONE

Life Begins

Our lives consist of several stages with seasons, growth, or dormancy, and includes phases throughout each stage. We come into the world at birth, and Scriptures give us a snapshot of how this takes place.

First, we are known by the Lord before we were ever created in our mother's womb.

> Proverbs 8:22-23:
> *"The Lord formed me from the beginning, before he created anything else. I was appointed in ages past, at the very first, before the earth began."*

Scripture tells us we were woven together in our mother's womb by the Lord Himself (Psalm 139:13). This beginning starts us thinking about how we're made. It reveals how all those individual qualities and talents came into being.

Knowing from Scripture that God knew us before the world was created was not something I had thought about much. We can read in the Book of Ephesians this very fact.

Ephesians 1:4:
"Even before he made the world, God loved us and chose us in Christ to be holy and without fault in his eyes."

He intricately put us together (created by God — woven) before our birth, and He knows us better than we know ourselves. We are not a mistake. We are individually created in His image and given a uniqueness like no other (Genesis 1:27; 5:1-2).

He knew us and knitted us together in our mother's womb, making us a creation of His — with a soul and spirit. According to Scriptures, this detail is also a reality, and evolution did not have any part in our existence (Colossians 1:15-17). Our life is a product of our Creator — God!

We marvel at snowflakes and how they can each be different. We identify people by their fingerprints because each imprint is distinct and uniquely different and identifiable. So unique even to the exactness of distinguishing one person from everyone else.

Our DNA can identify an individual with precision in today's world. We can learn our ancestry and those who lived before us that make up each generation and from where they evolved. This difference allows science to determine each individual's preciseness more clearly because of their specific physical characteristics.

God tells us in the bible this is how He created us individually. Now man can verify his existence on earth, which scientifically can be documented with preciseness and without confusion in our modern world.

Isn't it amazing how our continued findings line up with the Word of God. You would think someone designed all this, and we're just finding out it is real. Our findings on earth still continue to line up with the facts we find stated in the bible.

STAGE 1

This is Stage 1 of our lives. We are intricately put together by our Creator in our mother's womb and given physical life, personality, abilities, individuality, and created in likeness to God, our Creator. We are given a soul and spirit, and our physical existence begins the moment of conception. Over the nine-month period of gestation, we are woven into the individual person God has chosen us to become.

The preciseness and exactness is unlike any other in all of creation. God creates us as an individual person with similarities to other family members but still very different and unique. We are one of a kind — an individual that God has specifically assigned to life on earth with a specific purpose.

In one culture that I lived, the one-year-old celebration for an infant took place three months after their physical birth. That culture concluded that life began at conception, and, for this reason, a person's age started at that point rather than from physical delivery from the mother's womb.

I found this to be very interesting, and since learning that viewpoint, I continue to see why they came to that belief. If we could understand life to begin at conception, I wonder how likely abortion would ever have come into existence. Imagine that!

We are one human being, that exists, but there has not been one like you before, nor will there be another like you after your life on earth ends! You are one of a kind (a distinct person) that has been specifically designed for a designated time to fulfill God's purpose for your living.

The Lord tells us He has a plan, and we are a part of that plan. Should we decide to follow His leading that plan will unfold during our lifetime, and His purpose for us will reach a level beyond our abilities to achieve on our own! To me, this is quite a challenge to take on. But with His help, we can obtain all that He has planned for each of us!

Read the following Excerpts from Scripture and see for Yourself

> Jeremiah 29:11-13:
> *"For I know the plans I have for you," says the Lord. "They are plans for good and not for disaster, to give you a future and a hope. In those days when you pray, I will listen. If you look for me wholeheartedly, you will find me."*

> Psalm 40:5:
> *"O Lord my God, you have performed many wonders for us. Your plans for us are too numerous to list. You have no equal. If I tried to recite all your wonderful deeds, I would never come to the end of them."*

I find great comfort in reading that the God we serve has included me in His plans and will allow me to serve Him and be a part of what He is doing on the earth today. I'm not an accident but rather an individual that gets to participate and be a part of an extensive plan that He has orchestrated and put into action before the beginning of time.

STAGE 2

Once we are physically born, we enter the world from our mother's womb, we automatically enter Stage 2. A sinful nature accompanies our entrance into the world due to Adam and Eve's sin in the Garden of Eden (see Romans 5). This provides us with a body that our unique soul and spirit can reside while we're living.

After we are born, we enter the physical world as a breathing bundle of human flesh, having a body, soul, and spirit. Our body provides the vehicle that gives us functionality with our surrounds and allows us to operate with physical mobility, thinking, and a free will to choose for ourselves.

This entrance into Stage 2 of our lives is our physical birth. It is our beginning on earth, we become a living being, ready to start living outside our mother's womb and learning to deal with all the newness that comes once we enter this earthly domain in the flesh.

Our soul is our personality, consciousness, feelings, emotions, with expressions to follow with speech and a vocabulary to express ourselves. How all this comes together is very specific to each person. There are usually many similarities but also many differences, and depending on our formulated thinking, can vary dramatically.

Much care and attention are necessary to grow from a helpless baby on through childhood to adulthood. Years are required during this time for us to grow and learn the essentials to becoming mature and independent from our parents. We are learning all the time to develop a mental evaluation and guideline in which to formulate how to make the right decisions for ourselves. We function and are continually learning how to adapt to life while maintaining our feelings and emotions to remain acceptable and under control.

We learn to live life while making decisions and choices that we find to be of our particular interests. Special attention is necessary to grow during each season and continually progress on your journey to become a responsible, mature adult.

When we enter Stage 2, we quickly discover we have a body, mind, and a soul. Our body is our vehicle in which to live out our life on earth. It has been created in the likeness of God. It can adapt to our environment and has purposely been designed to make the journey in a physical world. Its function serves us while we're alive, giving us mobility and ability to operate to our fullness. Physical restrictions do apply, and our journey involves quite a few lumps and bumps.

Our mind is pretty much a blank sheet of paper. Still, in our development, it gathers all that is around us and begins to store and formulate decisions and opinions based on our environment, parent's reactions, discipline, situations encountered, learned responses, and of course, our individual disposition with its many responses and feelings of emotions stirring inside of us.

It is only natural to want the best for ourselves and seek what lies ahead with eagerness and a sense of excitement. The future holds so many new adventures, and our youth comes storming in like springtime with a new sense of enthusiasm that is exhilarating and much welcomed so we can see what we can do because of our very presence.

We learn to master our environment and exercise the many skills we have learned. Many seasons, phases, years of education, life experiences, failures, and successes occur during this time to enhance our progress and catapult us into maturity. Our youthful thinking believes it comes too slow according to our estimation, but it comes nevertheless.

The adults around us provide examples from which to draw our responses. We plan to become a person that handles life and prospers during our lifetime, doing what is rewarding, which exhibits our talents and produces achievements that surpass our dreams for the future.

Being born into a family brings with it characteristics that come from genetics, actions and reactions with our parents and loved ones we frequently are around. We have certain similarities, but we soon learn we have different ideas even though we are all based in the same environment.

We can be raised in the exact same environment and still grow up with many differences because we are so unique as individuals, but very much alike all at the same time. This uniqueness is present throughout our existence and provides us with many challenges and areas that we must endure.

For example, my sister and I both sneeze alike — it even sounds the same — the same in pitch and length, but we certainly are not alike. When we are tired, we walk similarly like our father. Our body build runs very much the same, and we attack projects with confidence and enthusiasm and see the project through to the end. We both are very determined.

We developed in different ways to resolve issues and answer many different questions differently. And like childhood, we both encountered very similar surroundings, but still, we usually don't see things the same way or have the same opinion.

We each had the same parents, same location of childhood, same one-room school of education for several years before moving to the city. Our gifts and talents were quite different, but our same environment produced similarities, but we still grew up very different.

Take another look and see an example of differences. My sister was taking a college class, and she was to make an abstract creation for her art class. Once she completed her flower creation out of metal and wire, it was beautiful in design and exhibited quite an artistic example of her creativity. But — it was not in any way an abstract example of art.

Her professor told her she needed to make some changes in her art creation if she intended to receive a favorable grade for the project not-to-mention for the semester's final grade. She had complained to me several times of what she could do to up her grade for this art piece.

Remember, our background was very similar, but our grown-up approach to problem-solving had developed in two very different directions. The different directions became evident as we discussed her not so abstract art project. Our different ideas regarding a solution became dramatically apparent as she permitted me to resolve her problem.

One evening I was visiting with her after a meal at her house. She was again telling me about her dilemma. I told her I could easily fix her beautiful art piece in short order without further delay. I told her it was a simple matter and would result in the kind of artwork her art class professor required and would get her a satisfactory grade.

She got up from the table and handed me her art project, and I immediately took it outside and placed it behind my car. As I backed over her beautiful art project, in her driveway, it immediately became 'abstract' right before her very eyes. I did not have the college education necessary to take on this project, but I had a good idea of how abstract was supposed to look. So I 'converted' her beautiful art piece in to an acceptable, unique piece of abstract art and resolved her problem.

The look on her face, the verbal scream of — *you have got to be kidding* — rose to a somewhat forced level of sound that I could hear inside the car with the windows up. I think a few neighbors also heard because the decibel level was probably around the sound of a loud lawnmower or a passing Harley without a muffler.

Once I pulled forward and ran over it again the 'redesign' was complete and took only a few minutes. It bothered me she got so upset because I was only doing what she had ask me to do — I had adapted her artwork to comply with her college art professor just as she had asked. Whew! Sibling rivalry has proven to be a significant challenge in my family ever since that minor event.

Anyway, she got an excellent grade on her 'abstract' creation and passed the course with compliments for her creativity and compliance to the specified instructions. She still relates back to my help, but now it is with laughter instead of a loud outburst of emotion and horror.

I thought my approach to resolve her issue would have been quite different from her immediate response. It seems our thinking, although based on very similar backgrounds, might have been more in line with each other, but obviously not!

Thank you Lord, I'm still able to go visit her. But — she never did ask me to help her with 'anything' (artwork) ever again. I did get to hang a couple of ceiling fans in her house in the years to follow, but things were never quite the same after that. I guess that once was spectacular enough, and there's no need to wow her ever again — ever in her lifetime!

That's enough of a good example of similar backgrounds but very different responses to life's many challenges. Now let's get back to the specific subject matter once again. We each have a 'footprint' in time left by our physical existence with a traceable path and a precise identification or 'mark' in history that only we could fill. I'm convinced we are positioned exactly in God's time plan and born right on schedule.

We each have been designed for such a time as this. So unique no one else could live our life any better in our place. We are a person so unique there is no one person like anyone else. We are individuality designed and never to be duplicated again.

Now, let's get into the biblical facts that accompany our entrance into Stage 2. The bible tells us each person enters the world at birth. This physical birth brings with it a curse due to the original sin committed by Adam and Eve in the Garden of Eden (Genesis 3:15).

We also learn our entrance automatically places us in a spiritual condition that's very unfavorable. What is that? It is a spiritual separation from God. This separation is called enmity, blocking our spirit from our Creator. So, from birth on, we are under that curse, which separates us from God spiritually.

This act of disobedience in the Garden placed each of us under a curse upon our arrival in Stage 2. This placement was automatic and carried a burden on our life inescapable without God's plan of Salvation. What is the plan? God's plan to resolve this issue was provided by sending His Son, Jesus, to the earth, and His death on the cross erased the curse that was a result of the original sin in the Garden.

In Reading Scripture from the Bible, we Learn How and Why

John 1:14:
"So the Word became human and made his home among us. He was full of unfailing love and faithfulness. And we have seen his glory, the glory of the Father's one and only Son."

Colossians 1:15-20:
"Christ is the visible image of the invisible God. He existed before anything was created and is supreme over

all creation, for through him God created everything in the heavenly realms and on earth."

"He made the things we can see and the things we can't see—such as thrones, kingdoms, rulers, and authorities in the unseen world. Everything was created through him and for him. He existed before anything else, and he holds all creation together."

"Christ is also the head of the church, which is his body. He is the beginning, supreme over all who rise from the dead. So he is first in everything."

"For God in all his fullness was pleased to live in Christ, and through him God reconciled everything to himself. He made peace with everything in heaven and on earth."

So, What did Jesus have to Do?

Philippians 2:6-8:
"Though he was God, he did not think of equality with God as something to cling to. Instead, he gave up his divine privileges; he took the humble position of a slave and was born as a human being. When he appeared in human form, he humbled himself in obedience to God and died a criminal's death on a cross."

Jesus had to Die as a Human Being to Break the Power of the Devil

Hebrews 2:14:
"Because God's children are human beings—made of flesh and blood—the Son also became flesh and blood. For only as a human being could he die, and only by dying could he break the power of the devil, who had the power of death."

Why Couldn't we Die for our Sins?

1 Timothy 2:5:
"For, There is one God and one Mediator who can reconcile God and humanity—the man Christ Jesus."

Was Jesus God in the Flesh — Really?

Colossians 2:9:
"For in Christ lives all the fullness of God in a human body."

When is the Right Time for Salvation?

2 Corinthians 6:2:
For God says, "At just the right time, I heard you. On the day of salvation, I helped you." Indeed, the "right time" is now. Today is the day of salvation.

How do we Earn our Salvation?

Ephesians 2:9:
"Salvation is not a reward for the good things we have done, so none of us can boast about it."

Romans 3:27:
"Can we boast, then, that we have done anything to be accepted by God? No, because our acquittal is not based on obeying the law. It is based on faith."

Romans 4:2:
"If his good deeds had made him acceptable to God, he would have had something to boast about. But that was not God's way."

Where is Salvation Found?

Psalm 27:1:
"The Lord is my light and my salvation— so why should I be afraid? The Lord is my fortress, protecting me from danger, so why should I tremble?"

Psalm 50:23:
"But giving thanks is a sacrifice that truly honors me. If you keep to my path, I will reveal to you the salvation of God."

Psalm 62:2:
"He alone is my rock and my salvation, my fortress where I will never be shaken."

Psalm 74:12:
"You, O God, are my king from ages past, bringing salvation to the earth."

Psalm 79:9:
"Help us, O God of our salvation! Help us for the glory of your name. Save us and forgive our sins for the honor of your name."

Psalm 103:17:
"But the love of the Lord remains forever with those who fear him. His salvation extends to the children's children."

That human form was Jesus and His death on the cross satisfied God's penalty for sin and provided a way to escape our unfavorable condition. How? By having faith in God's solution and believing what Christ did so we could come out from under the sin penalty caused by Adam and Eve's disobedience in the Garden.

This situation causes us consequences that must be approached biblically to get resolved. Man has sought to find a way on his own since time began but has never or ever will find a way to solve this disconnection with God on his own.

As I said, since we are born into this Stage 2, we are automatically born into sin and its consequences. This is a fact and is a reality that applies to all humanity. Scripture tells us this is our starting point when we're born into the world. It is the beginning of our life here on earth without being *housed* in the womb of another person. Since it is the same for each person born into the world, our physical existence, as we know it, begins here.

Life in Stage 2 can be approached in two different ways. There are only two choices available, and they are:

1. Leave our spiritual situation the way it is and remain in Stage 2.
2. Choose to remove ourselves from Stage 2 by believing in God's option — by accepting His Salvation.

Choice 1 — Leave everything just the way it is and live out your life and ignore the consequences of sin in which you were born. This choice keeps you in Stage 2 and assures you that Stage 3 is next.

Choice 2 — Is to choose the option God provided and live your life by faith in the Son of God. Believing that Jesus's death, burial, and resurrection and all He accomplished by dying on the cross and paying for our sin debt before we physically die and enter into eternity.

No matter our choice, we will mature and grow into adulthood. The results of our selection will begin to either grow us in the Lord or not. Our progression to the age of accountability and adulthood will occur. Then we have continued opportunities to choose which stage is next and where we want to focus our attention.

We didn't have a choice when we entered Stage 1, but the Lord made a way that will give us an option to resolve this curse of sin we live and entered through physical birth. This fact does directly affect our future and the next stage we will occupy. As soon as we understand this fact and its consequences, we can make the choice to move past the negative final results.

I don't have an exact age that would designate when our accountability would start, but I do believe there is a time. That time is when we distinguish right from wrong and understand we are responsible for our decisions. It takes place in our early years and marks a time of decision from that point on based on our conscience and how we respond.

When I Look at Scripture I Find

> James 4:17:
> *"Remember, it is sin to know what you ought to do and then not do it."*

I believe our conscience develops as we learn and grow from birth. There is a time when we become acutely aware of the difference. The presence of the Lord is evident through the Holy Spirit in the world today. Our gathering information through teaching, reading the Word, hearing a biblical sermon, following the example of others, godly correction, instruction, and preaching in righteousness surround us constantly. We are continually becoming aware of the difference between right and wrong, as each of us encounters life during our early years.

Nature provides much to see the direct results of God's creation, and the idea of order and the obvious realization of His creativity is evident in everything. Scripture tells us that each person is provided the beauty of nature to experience our Creator God. Our earthly surroundings offer an example of His handiwork. From this we each witness He exists and that He created our environment because it is obviously everywhere around us. Our environment is an example set before us to witness evidence of God's existence (Romans 1:20).

Adam and Eve were given instructions of what was okay and what to avoid. At this point, they were sinless before the Lord. Once they chose to disobey, knowing it was wrong but did it anyway, then they sinned. It was a conscious decision, and each willfully decided to disobey.

When Adam told God that — *the woman you gave me made me do it* — this attempt to blame didn't produce a good excuse, and he discovered the consequences of his sin immediately in real-time. The conscientious guilt of sin was a new awareness never before fully realized. The severity of their sin was now convicting them and what it would cause. But, because they started believing a lie they fell into sin, choosing what they wanted more than obeying God.

They allowed themselves to follow after their fleshly desires and do what they wanted because they were curious to discover on their own. They both responded to the temptation and sin followed. Once the sin was acted out, we learn they both became immediately aware of their sin evident as they quickly hid from God (Genesis 3:8).

Why? Because they immediately knew what they had done was wrong and because their emotions and feelings were directly affected. They were ashamed to stand in God's presence now and had never felt this way before they suffered the consequences of their decision. They deliberately chose to act in direct disobedience to what God had told them to avoid. Their deliberate act of disobedience was a sin, and the consequences followed.

We do the same thing today. Deliberately making a wrong choice because we choose to is sin. Knowing it's wrong, but doing it anyway is a choice. If we do something and don't know it's wrong, then it is not yet sinning. Choosing to do wrong and acting it out makes us accountable for the sin we committed, and there is always a consequence.

Something to take into consideration — doing what is right also has direct consequences, and the rewards for obedience are blessings. Our actions will reap what we sow. All seed will reproduce a crop of its kind. We would all like to see the results of a good crop immediately, but for a bad crop — not ever. Unlike our choice to sin, our choice to obey brings godly fruit and builds Christlike character in us all simultaneously (2 Peter 1:3-8). This process of obedience will yield a great harvest as a direct result.

This fallen stage we were born into is not our doom because God has provided a way to escape its negative consequences. But, if this condition is left to itself, we will suffer the results and will, at life's end, reap the results causing us to enter into Stage 3.

Believing God is our Creator is a spiritual truth. It is not only a scriptural truth regarding creation, but it's a fact our findings on earth reveal. If you believe the bible is the written truth revealed to humanity from God, that's great. If you believe only parts of the bible that is quite another issue.

Even cults reflect certain truths written in God's Word, but they veer off onto twisted trails that sound good to our natural minds. The nuggets of Truth then become tainted with lies that sound good but are contrary to the whole truth. These variations then become strongholds that stand against God's message to humanity and lead some people astray. That's why we are warned against them.

The Lord is not blind to these lies; else He would not give us warning. Our relationship with Him is critical, so we should continue to seek His wisdom and call on Him for help. Twisted truth is not unusual since the devil has used this tactic beginning in the Garden of Eden. When we choose to believe only what we agree with regarding the bible, we close ourselves to the whole truth found in the bible. Partial truth leaves room for untruth, and we see this everyday in the world we live in.

Check out an example of believing in something that is contrary to the truth found in Scripture. The theory of evolution has been referenced and taught as the origin of all humanity. The creator of this theory was Charles Darwin and he himself set guidelines to determine if it was factual. Darwin stated what evidence was necessary to prove his theory as accurate. That's why it was called a theory.

The guideline determined by Darwin had hopes that future fossil findings would prove his theory to be correct. Upon his death in 1896, he was hopeful his theory would prove itself out. But, today, no further evidence has supported his theory. Thus, it is still a theory — not fact!

Since Darwin's theory did not receive any support based on future fossil findings, its validity cannot be substantiated. The fact that no fossils have been discovered to prove his ideas, then Darwin himself determined his theory to be false without evidence.

Somehow the world grasp his theory, rather than the bible, regarding evolution, and our world has treated it as fact rather than basing his theory on the fossil finding discovered over time from studies of the earth's history. Since no fossil findings provide evidence to support Darwin's origin of man — it is not a fact. It is still a theory because the earth's findings do not support this type of origin.

Both Darwin's theory and his conclusion regarding the validity were based on expected future fossil findings to become historical facts. Since Evolution is a theory, not a fact, and our past geological records verifies just that — why do we persist in calling it factual? A theory without factual backing remains only a theory. It provides evidence that Creation, as described in the bible, seems to be more valid because there is no evidence against its validity like there is against evolution.

I want our school systems to present both the Bible and Darwin's Theory to our education system so children can learn all the facts from each approach to explaining creation. I believe teaching the bible would offer a much better explanation of creation and how it took place according to Scripture as compared to our findings on the earth.

Teaching a theory as fact to our children in schools continues to undermine the facts found regarding the origin of possibilities to the next generation. We are selling an untruth as fact that promotes continual disillusion to all foundational learning blocks that form our natural thinking. Secular reasoning in our natural thinking is then limited and without the possibility of obtaining actual evidence or continued learning.

Isn't education to present the current knowledge man has learned? Don't we want our next generation to think and decide for themselves? What if the bible is true as God's Word states in the biblical history of man and all creation? Aren't we missing the opportunity to present to our children an education they deserve without a bias approach?

I see in Scriptures where creation (humankind) provides evidence of its Creator. The mindset of humankind to believe otherwise is a lie and distracts from what took place. Today we give a fairy tale alternative that confuses the truth and eliminate God from what took place.

Then, to dismiss the bible because it was written so long ago and has no purpose today in its applications and principles is absurd. I have discovered the bible to be extremely advantageous and very helpful in living life on earth to the fullest.

I've found solutions and answers to life's challenges that helped immensely in solving personal issues, problems, and providing instructions that proved out beneficial. As I grow and mature, I learn that science continues to discover evidence that is in agreement with biblical creation and continues to find more validity than previous generations.

I discovered the scriptural principles' results were so effective that repeated usage had changed my life for the better, no matter the problem. Does that sound too old and outdated to be unusable or ineffective in its entirety? Should I rule out its results of repeated success because the source is too old or deemed outdated?

Doesn't wisdom prove itself to be true over time (Luke 7:35)? When we apply some theory that continues to work, over and over, doesn't this testing give evidence that the validity in application and results are then proven and factual? Yes, this repeated finding is then proven true because it works and yields an end result that can be repeated with certainty? A theory with 100% end results would then becomes a fact. What's your deduction?

Job 12:13:
"But true wisdom and power are found in God; counsel and understanding are his."

Maybe that's why the bible is so powerful. It provides principles of wisdom that repeatedly resolve the issue for which they were intended. Experience this outcome for yourself and enjoy the results each and every time.

Scripture tells us where we can find wisdom (Proverbs 2:6). Wisdom is the smartest thing you can do (Proverbs 4:7). Wisdom can add years to your life (Proverbs 9:11). Again I ask — *why would anyone select a theory over a fact?*

Isn't what has been proven over time and is evident in the earth's fossil history evidence of past events? These findings should be viewed most definitely above a possible theory of what happened that sounds good but cannot be substantiated with any evidence or geological proof it originated this way?

I do realize this subject matter raises many arguments and that we teach evolution in our schools. I also understand that when put to the test of time, evolution does not live up to the elevation we place it in our education system.

I believe the bible clearly states our origin, and we can choose to accept it or not. Or not, puts one on shaky ground that is not supported by any facts. Believing by faith places us on the foundation sited by the Bible as truth!

We can see that evolution is a theory which earthly facts do not support. Believing in Creation, as God describes, takes faith in something we cannot see (Hebrews 11:1 & 6). If we approach the origin of man with a closed mind, we discard the facts found today in our earth's history.

If we choose to avoid or approach this matter with a closed mind, we put learning and understanding at a point of limited possibilities. Learning never stops, so if we chose to close our minds, then we are presenting willful closure to any further education. This mindset is willful ignorance, which is translated into stupidity when the final results are gathered all together.

This dilemma exists to this day, but it can be resolved through faith for a believer in the Lord and what the bible tells us. I choose to take my information from the bible and see truth as the Word of God has spoken through man and provided for our instruction, correction, knowledge and wisdom as revealed in:

> 2 Timothy 3:16-17:
> *"All Scripture is given by inspiration of God, and is profitable for doctrine, for reproof, for correction, for instruction in righteousness, that the man of God may be complete, thoroughly equipped for every good work."*

God is the creator of man and made each person in the image of Himself. This statement is found in Scripture (Genesis 1:26) and is proven in the fossil findings man has discovered through his search on earth.

Do you really think that a single cell came into existence alone and developed into a complicated, multi-functional human being? A being able to think, have a soul, a mind to learn, and reproduce a being so intricate its existence could rise to the level of a human-being on its own?

If it was to develop and grow alone, how did it exist until it could stand alone and evolve through trial and error? Each trial and error in development until it could stand alone would have resulted in death, after death for each cell all along the way. How could it be dead and somehow come to life again and exist? How would something dead re-create itself? Evolution? I don't think so.

Creation? The most probable way ANYTHING could come into existence and be so intricately put together in such detail is way beyond self-evolving. We humans have been around quite a few years and still don't understand the human body. Could we re-create life after all these years of experience? It appears to me it takes more faith to believe in the theory of evolution than Creation when all the facts are laid out on the table.

In our society, we refer to a doctor having a practice. This profession takes a tremendous amount of education and internship to meet the requirement necessary to accomplish the honorable title doctor. It is an amazing amount of education, and work to earn this title and practice this profession.

I'm sure you've heard jokes about the reason it is called a practice, but consider the physical nature of human beings. This is an unbelievably complicated creation, and understanding every aspect of its intricate function is so beyond humankind we must learn about its complicated components and how they function with a multitude of variables and reasons and determine why they react as they do.

Do you believe that humanity could recreate itself today with all that we know from our past? Of course, there are generalities and functions that are termed primary and general in their purpose internally, but there are also many ailments we do not know the cause, nor do we know their cure.

Just think, even a common cold does not have a cure — we only treat the symptoms. Then consider the knowledge of many doctor's today, which is absolutely impressive. They still don't know how to create life or anything even close that's human and functions as a whole person does from birth.

Our progress over time has been amazing and is a credit to the medical field in their ability to perform and bring healing to those of us needing help just to survive and function normally. I greatly appreciate the intelligence and dedication necessary to become a doctor and the many forms of medicine and procedures they preform and accomplish.

I would not be alive today without doctors that were able to correct the many difficulties experienced in my lifetime. I am grateful to the Lord for guiding them to become apart of His healing team. They are called to this profession and administer great miracles in making life better for all of us.

It took a Creator to bring all we experience together in such elaborate fashion. It took an intelligence way beyond our intelligence, or any combination of cell reproduction, to evolve into what we see and experience today. And, we are still way behind to even imagine that we could create or believe that this universe appeared out of nothing.

Read Job 38:4 through Job 40:5 and determine who the Creator was of the world we live in today. These verses of Scripture answer questions you may have never before thought about in such detail. I was certainly amazed, and it was a part of my decision-making to view our Creation from a biblical perspective.

CHAPTER TWO

Life Ending Without God

STAGE 2

S tage 2 is where we live out our earthly existence and journey through life until death comes knocking. That's when our physical existence will end. At this end, our soul and spirit will automatically move into Stage 3. Our death without God automatically projects us into eternity. When no choice during our lifetime was made for Salvation, Hades is our eternal destination.

This stage is just living life without God as a nonbeliever. We struggle through life without His help or assistance and continue believing that there is no more to life than existing. We just travel alone and learn to function and survive on our strength. We are living to somehow get through based on our intellect, wisdom, and understanding. Existing independently is only existence — that's all, and there can be much more to living life with God.

Have you ever talked with someone who believe's he's just unlucky in life? This person will tell you that if I had some good breaks like so and so had or would have been born into a wealthy family, life would have been much better. That didn't happen, so I'm stuck in this place that I am without any good fortune or luck to change things and improve my life.

This kind of life is a dismal place, but I'll get through somehow just you wait and see. Maybe I can win a few bucks and hit the lottery or strike it rich if someone in my family hits an oil well in Oklahoma. That will take me up to another level of living and would suit me just fine. Why, I might have a rich relative who will leave me an inheritance. Could be — right?

An example from Scripture gives a story of a life in Stage 2 without any regard for a future in eternity. There is no concern for others struggling in life. In this story, the person is convinced they are okay because their comfortable life indicates that status and wealth are good indicators that everything is better than satisfactory. What do you think?

Take a Look at the following Biblical Account

> Luke 16:19-31:
> *Jesus said, "There was a certain rich man who was splendidly clothed in purple and fine linen and who lived each day in luxury."*
>
> *"At his gate lay a poor man named Lazarus who was covered with sores. As Lazarus lay there longing for scraps from the rich man's table, the dogs would come and lick his open sores."*
>
> *"Finally, the poor man died and was carried by the angels to be with Abraham. The rich man also died and was buried,"*
>
> *"And his soul went to the place of the dead. There, in torment, he saw Abraham in the far distance with Lazarus at his side."*

"The rich man shouted, 'Father Abraham, have some pity! Send Lazarus over here to dip the tip of his finger in water and cool my tongue. I am in anguish in these flames."

"But Abraham said to him, 'Son, remember that during your lifetime you had everything you wanted, and Lazarus had nothing. So now he is here being comforted, and you are in anguish.'"

"And besides, there is a great chasm separating us. 'No one can cross over to us from there.' Then the rich man said, 'Please, Father Abraham, at least send him to my fathers's home.'"

"For I have five brothers, and I want him to warn them so they don't end up in this place of torment."

How did the rich man enter eternity? He left his results to chance and spent his existence enjoying the good life on earth in Stage 2 without any regard for his eternal destination. Basing eternity's destination on your standard of living on earth will yield false thinking and eternal doom.

If we leave our destiny to fate and believe that whatever comes will happen no matter what we say or do — the results are fatal. The rich man had a good life on earth; he was rich, well clothed, and lived in luxury. But — that did not ensure or reflect his destiny!

It is quite evident he did not care about other less fortunate folks and did not help anyone during his lifetime. He thought he was doing fine without God's help, so he did not make any arrangement for life after death Our level of comfort in life is not a barometer for the afterlife.

The rich man failed to realize that his comfort and wealth came from God and assumed that this placed him above others. This assumption proved out to be a major error. Humankind sometimes thinks that our status in life is a sign of favor from the Lord or that we can do just fine on our own without any godly assistance.

Pride can lead us astray, and that worldly logic and thinking may convince us we're on the right path because life is treating us so well. Living an abundant life, well dressed and well-fed are not necessarily signs of success as the Lord views success.

As you can see from the story in Luke, the rich man ended up in an unwanted place of torment, where the souls of the godless end up after life on earth. A place of anguish and thirst. Putting yourself in the rich man's place and knowing there is no way out is quite haunting. He wasn't even able to get Father Abraham to send Lazarus back from the dead to warn his five brothers or give him any relief to his thirst.

Father Abraham told the rich man that there is ample warning of what lies ahead once death comes during our lifetime. And, we each will die and leave this earthly domain for eternity — to somewhere. Our soul and spirit will leave this mortal body and either go to be with the Lord or into Eternal damnation, as explained by the rich man in the Gospel of Luke you just read.

The location of life after death is a choice each of us must make in Stage 2. By doing nothing, we will join the rich man in his eternal doom where the fiery lake of burning sulfur will eternally burn, and all who enter will be tormented day and night forever and ever (Revelation 20:10). A place without any way to escape — ever. The time to choose your eternal destination is now before your life on earth ends! After your life on earth ends — it's too late!

Leaving life to chance is similar to the 40-year trip through the desert by the Israelites as Moses led them. God intended to lead them to the Promised Land, which God had prepared for their pleasure and enjoyment. (Read the Book of Exodus to understand what took place as God led the Israelites out of Egypt.)

God had appointed Moses to lead His People, the Israelites, and deliver them from their slavery in Egypt, which had existed for 400-years. Their exodus from Egypt took them out of slavery and on an 11-day journey to the Promised Land. God was taking them to a plentiful and pleasurable location that would provide for their practical needs with the greatest of ease.

The problem then became apparent they were enslaved to their own way of thinking and were not open to a change for a better life planned by God. They refused to believe God and His plan for them. And their lack of faith resulted in them struggling through life rather than accepting and follow God.

Why the problem? Because now they needed to yield to their new slave master — God. Instead, they chose to depend on their thinking and reasoning. As a result, they traveled for 40-years, not believing in God and added years to the God-planned 11-day journey. They moaned and murmured the whole trip and refused to put their faith in the Creator. They were stubborn — like a mule! Know anybody like that?

Now keep in mind God provided all their food and water in a climate that had no food or water available. Somehow, the miracles they experienced did not affect their thinking or cause them to believe or cooperate with the Creator. God operating in their mist did nothing to change their minds. The undeniable miracles they lived with were viewed with disregard.

The stubborn Israelites were a people not even thankful for the miracles they witnessed as they traveled. Miracles that allowed their existence to continue and provisions to be provided that were required to continue on their journey. It is hard to understand their frame of mind and the decisions they made. They experienced more difficulties and hardships during the entire trip because they refused to follow after God.

They had a Cloud to protect them from the sun's heat during the day, which changed to a Pillar of Fire by night to protect them from the night elements. These unusual signs were obvious, so doubt could not be an excuse not to believe God was present.

Nevertheless, they were disobedient to God's leading while the whole time depended on Him to keep them fed, clothed, watered, protected, just to survive the harsh elements they were existing in — the desert!

This 40-year trip could have been made in 11-days had they chosen to believe in God and follow His directions. After the 11-days, the intent was that the problematic desert travel would bring them to the Promised Land and place them in a land described as 'milk and honey'.

What existed there was a people the Lord would cause the Israelites to conquer in battle and receive all that God had intended from the plentiful spoils that awaited them. This was their destiny on earth during their lifetime if they would but follow God.

As a result, God allowed the unbelieving to die in the desert while Joshua and Caleb taught the next generation about the God they served. It took the long journey to let all those stubborn, non-believing folks perish in their disbelief. So, they died in their doubt without reaching God's plan and purpose for their lives.

They perished without seeing what God had in store for their future, which would have been very fulfilling and a blessing to them and their families. Their fate could have been bright and fulfilling with hope for the future generations that would follow them.

Everything they needed awaited them, but they're stubbornness and complaining blocked their way. They died without receiving the rewards God intended to prosper them with, as well as, His many blessings that would follow obedience.

The choice of disobedience to God's direction in life took them the challenging and hopeless journey. It caused them to suffer unnecessarily and struggle excessively during their existence on earth. Refusing God's help all along the way led to their failure and never reaching the purpose God had intended for them. It is no different for the stubborn and disobedient today.

Please keep in mind we're talking about 2-3 million Israelites, a massive group of people with enormous needs, and no way to get supplies except from God. The challenge to make an 11-day trip is enormous enough, but 40-years?

The point being, they chose not to believe and lived out their lives in a place, the desert, that could have been avoided by believing in the God. He was leading them to a *land of promise* that would have been manifested had they been obedient and believed.

The Israelites chose to remain stubborn when an option was available to get out of this desolate lifestyle. They remained stuck in the desert rather than opt-out and get into the Promised Land. We have the same choice today. Want help on your journey through life, or do you want to remain in the desert?

They chose a life without the Lord and doing life on their own. We have to reach a level of maturity in life to make our own decisions. Our choice to reject the Lord will causes us to remain in a stage that is considered desert because it is dry, uncomfortable, without exerting any faith in our Creator and doing life without any of His help. Welcome to Stage 2.

Why struggle alone? God did not equip us to travel life independently. And when we choose to do it by ourselves, He does not provide any help during our journey. He awaits our decision to ask for His help so He can provide what we need to flourish. All the while, He is just waiting on us to decide.

Going it alone is a time of complaining how difficult life is and that life is so unfair and burdensome. Stage 2 is very tough without the Lord, but God allows us to choose because He has made us with a free spirit. He has given us a free will to choose as we desire.

We can choose how to spend our life. We are given an option to this mundane existence without Him, but it is not forced on us — we need to choose for ourselves (Hebrews 5:9; 1 Peter 1:9). He's a request away from giving us the help we need.

Our existence through life as we journey without the Lord can be long and challenging, just like the Israelites. If we live without exerting any faith in what the bible is tellings us, we will struggle excessively as we trudge forward. Steadily moving toward the end of life with no chance for a better existence. This kind of life choice avoids all the blessings God intends.

It also eliminates Heaven from our destination of where to spend eternity. Choosing not to believe in God for our salvation, and remaining unwilling to utilize His principles makes for a laborious journey.

Do you ever wonder why your life is so difficult? Do you wonder why the good breaks never seem to come your way? Do you think Christianity is a belief for wimps that can't handle life on their own? Maybe you should rethink your opinion and selection.

Come on, get it out of your thinking and listen to yourself talk. Expressing what you really believe is the beginning of a better understanding how you feel and think. Realizing how we are as a person, how we think or believe, is critical to reaching an evaluation and understanding of why we think the way we do.

Continuing on with the Lord's help is how we get into the Promised Land utilizing God's provisions and arriving in life to a better place. Heaven isn't our Promised Land — living here, implementing His Word into our lives is our Promised Land! Life with God provides many opportunities unavailable from any other source.

Traveling alone, it will be a time of complaining how difficult life is and wondering if this is all there is to living? Well, no, it isn't. There is a great deal more! It is only a choice away and awaits our pursuit to receive all that God has planned for our lives.

A good question to ask is — In what stage of life have you chosen to reside? Take a good look and check out your current existence. How is life going for you now, and what are your plans for eternity? It is critical that you choose both before it's too late. This is something we each should think with serious consideration. We're either ready or we are not!

Remember, God allows us to choose because He has made us that way. God created us the way we are on purpose. We are given a free will so that we can decide for ourselves. We choose how to spend life, and we choose where to spend eternity.

Yes, we are given an option to improve this existence on earth and where we want to spend eternity, but it is not forced on us — we need to choose (Deuteronomy 3:19; 2 Kings 18:32; Jeremiah 38:20). Again, these are serious decisions and must be based on biblical facts, not necessarily on what you may think or what you have been told.

The bible tells us that miracles are all around us that speak to our existence in many ways. Viewing the heavens and all the stars is a witness to us that God exhibits (Nehemiah 9:6; Psalm 8:3). Scripture tells us He has named each star in existence and can call them by name (Isaiah 40:26). We learn that He placed each star you see in it location.

We are told we are surrounded by His creation that tells us He exists (Romans 1:20). This fact is revealed to all humanity and is undeniable. How? We can see, hear, smell, taste, feel, and experience it all. I certainly don't understand how all this is possible, but the bible tells me so, and I choose to believe it. My choice!

His witness (miracles) to creation is all around. Sometimes I believe we tend to marvel at the creation and ignore the Creator. The creation reveals His power and that He exists. He created it all, so ask yourself, how is this possible? We must believe by faith or reject it altogether.

As we journey on in Stage 2, we continue to observe and learn more about the world in which we live. We learn about new and exciting facts about our planet, outer space, our massive oceans, and are still discovering creatures in the sea that are entirely new to us.

We learn new methods for treating the human body and, at present, are developing types of medications that show promise in treating different cancers with research that can develop a 'cocktail' of medicine to stop it from resulting in death. Cancer was once viewed as certain death, but research has eliminated its fatal consequences in many cases.

As we venture forward, life brings with it adventures that bring added opportunities never before experienced. Opportunities to rely on the Lord's help and move on through our life to better our understanding and improve our scriptural knowledge. In Stage 2, we discover from the bible that the physical body dies, and only our Soul and Spirit move on into eternity.

Once Stage 2 ends in physical death, the unsaved soul and spirit enter Stage 3, which is Eternal damnation, or Hades. Scripture provides this picture of our existence after this physical life ends on earth. It is not a pretty picture we see from Scripture, for one that is unsaved.

Our earthly physical body is not designed, nor can it exist in eternity. Our soul and spirit can, but they require a new container. Once death in our earthly body arrives, we are given a spiritual form that can survive in eternity. Our life here on earth is only temporary, but eternity is forever. This forever eternity, we all will enter, never ends, and our chosen destination will be where we spend it.

Upon death, this would conclude life on earth, and choosing not to follow after God, places us into Eternal damnation automatically. Since there are two places provided to spend eternity, we have the power to choose where to spend ours.

Giving us a choice is one reason for Jesus coming and dying on the cross to provide an option for us so we can exit Stage 2, skipping over Stage 3 altogether, and enter Stage 4 — saved and without fear of Eternal damnation. And, secure in knowing we will spend eternity with the Lord!

Choosing this option is God's way to save humanity from the consequences of the original sin committed in the Garden of Eden. God's plan to resolve the fall of humankind is freely offered to everyone. According to the Scriptures, all we must do is accept His plan and believe by faith in His Son (Romans 10:9-10).

So What's the Point?

As I said earlier, life without Christ is a desert way of living. Life with Christ is the Promised Land furnished with His help and provisions. We reach a new level of how to live life and benefit through Christ, which we could not obtain independently. The power of God in our lives changes everything! Nothing remains hopeless or lost, or without Heaven as the final destination.

Choosing Jesus Christ as your Savior and Lord make everything He has accomplished on the Cross possible. This option is very exciting, and it illuminates multiple opportunities during our lifetime that are not reachable without Him as Lord of your life.

This option is terrific, and it takes place during our lifetime that is not reachable without Him. Our choices do make all the difference. Scripture gives us a picture of how to choose the best for our life on earth. Check out Deuteronomy given below:

> Deuteronomy 30:15-19:
> *"Now listen! Today I am giving you a choice between life and death, between prosperity and disaster. For I command you this day to love the LORD your God and keep his commands, decrees, and regulations by walking in his ways. If you do this, you will live and multiply, and the LORD your God will bless you and the land you are about to enter and occupy."*
>
> *"But if your heart turns away and you refuse to listen, and if you are drawn away to serve and worship other gods, then I warn you now that you will certainly be destroyed. You will not live a long, good life in the land your are crossing the Jordan to occupy."*
>
> *"Today I have given you a choice between life and death, between blessings and curses. Now I call on heaven and earth to witness the choice you make. Oh, that you would choose life, so that you and your descendants might live!"*

Choosing Him is the desire of God's heart for everyone and has been before the very beginning of humanity. God knows what we are capable of doing, and because He has given us a choice, we are free to choose for ourselves. He's hoping we will understand the difference between life and death and choose life with Him.

What Does the Lord Say?

> Psalm 32:8:
> *The Lord says, "I will guide you along the best pathway for your life. I will advise you and watch over you."*

Proverbs 4:10:
"My child, listen to me and do as I say, and you will have a long, good life."

Proverbs 4:13:
"Take hold of my instruction; don't let them go. Guard them, for they are the key to life."

Proverbs 14:27:
"Fear of the LORD is a life-giving fountain; it offers escape from the snares of death."

As I keep saying, each of us have been given a free will. We have all been given a choice as to what kind of life we want to live, and He has provided the bible with instructions and principles for our benefit. The instruction manual He provided comes in many versions and can be heard should your reading skills be hampered in any way. Today we even have translations in most languages and also written in braille. Almost everyone can learn for themselves how to live a good life.

If you're serious about following after the Lord, there are churches, fellowships, and even underground groups in countries that forbid Christianity. The internet has a massive amount of information available for those having access. Almost every kind of book is available on the internet to bless and enhance our existence, and guide us to a better way to live life.

A library of reference books, interlinear translations, translations provided for comparison to another, cross-references, commentaries, dictionaries, languages, audio, TV, radio programs, teachings, ebooks, chat groups, bible studies, subjects to select with study guides, etc. All is available to those seeking to learn about the Lord and His principles, teachings, and examples. All provided for our consumption and continued learning.

A vast amount of information is readily available today. Most people can research a specific subject and find more information than we need to approach life from a scriptural perspective with little effort.

My Question is — What are You Waiting on?

Spoon feeding is not mentioned in the bible for our intake of His Word. Since we have access to so much today, we have little to no excuse for not knowing about the Lord. It's available for a very good reason. Like I said — What are you waiting on?

Take a look at selected Scriptures and see the option made available by God for our training and ability to receive His Wisdom:

The Reason for Jesus Coming to Earth

> John 3:16:
> *"For God loved the world so much that he gave his one and only Son, so that everyone who believes in him will not perish but have eternal life."*

Believing by Faith in Jesus ensures Eternal Life

> John 3:36:
> *"And anyone who believes in God's Son has eternal life. Anyone who doesn't obey the Son will never experience eternal life but remains under God's angry judgment."*

> John 5:24:
> *"I tell you the truth, those who listen to my message and believe in God who sent me have eternal life. They will never be condemned for their sins, but they have already passed from death to into life."*

Scripture Doesn't Save Anyone — Only Faith in Christ Does

John 5:39:
"You search the Scriptures because you think they give you eternal life. But the Scriptures point to me."

John 6:40:
"For it is my Father's will that all who see his Son and believe in him should have eternal life. I will raise them up at the last day."

John 14:6:
Jesus told him, *"I am the way, the truth, and the life. No one can come to the Father except through me."*

John 20:31:
"But these are written so that you may continue to believe that Jesus is the Messiah, the Son of God, and that <u>by believing in him you will have life by the power of his name</u>."

As you digest the above Scriptures, you can see your part in obtaining Salvation and Eternity in Heaven for yourself is quite simple. It is an act of obedience in faith by responding to God's Word. <u>It is the only opportunity available in our life that will save us</u> from Stage 3.

I say again, the bible tells us that the sins we were born into at birth is a sin that was brought on by Adam and Eve when they disobeyed God in the Garden of Eden. Scripture also tells us there is a way out of this dilemma, and it is explained below:

1 Corinthians 15:20-22:
"But in fact, Christ has been raised from the dead. He is the first of a great harvest of all who have died. So you see, just as death came into the world through a man. (Adam), now the resurrection from the dead has begun through another man (Jesus Christ.) Just as everyone dies because we all belong to Adam, everyone who belongs to Christ will be given new life."

The following prayer provides the bridge necessary to 'passover' Stage 3 and removes Eternal damnation from your final destination in eternity. If you're reading this book and don't know the Lord, you're in Stage 2. If you die tonight you will enter Stage 3.

Like I said a few paragraphs before, life without Christ is the desert. Life with Christ is our Promised Land. We reach a new level of how to live life and benefit through Christ what we could not obtain on our own.

The power of God in our lives changes everything! Nothing remains hopeless or lost or without heaven as the final destination. Choosing Jesus the Christ and what He has accomplished on the Cross is what makes all this possible.

This option is very exciting, and it illuminates opportunities during our lifetime what was not reachable without Him as Lord of your life. So, consider your position in Christ and accept His choice before your time runs out. I would highly recommend you take inventory regarding your status with the Lord and accept His solution before your death door slams.

How do you accept His offer of Salvation? I thought you would never ask. It can be completed in one prayer. Your choice can be made as you pray out loud, so you can hear yourself. His hearing is just fine but yours may need a little help to get through.

This prayer is simple, but repeating it to the Lord is you making your choice now to spend eternity with Him. Don't expect to understand every little detail, but do know this prayer will save your soul and release the Spirit of God into your spirit and you can experience Him, God, Jesus, the Holy Spirit for yourself.

This is Your Solution

Pray out Loud to the Lord:

Jesus, I am a sinner. I am sorry for all that I have done wrong. I repent of the sins in my life (lying, stealing, cursing, lusting, coveting, jealousy, hatefulness, what I was born into, etc) and I accept what you

(Jesus) did by dying on the cross in my place. I ask you to come into my heart and 'change me' into a 'new creation'. Give me the spiritual eyes to see and the ability to hear your voice as you take me on the path that you have planned for me even before the beginning of time. Cleanse me by your shed blood and fill me with your Holy Spirit. I want to serve you and grow into the person you created me to be. Help me be all that I was created for and to fulfill my destiny in you. I ask this in Jesus' name, Amen.

CHAPTER THREE

Who Signed Me Up For This?

This choice to accept Christ as your Lord takes you from Stage 2, and causes you to pass over Stage 3, and relocates you instantly into Stage 4. This stage places you in God's hands, and assures your eternity will be spent with Him. You are now a child of God, and all the benefits Christ obtained by dying in our place on the cross are made available. This package deal is extended to all humanity. It is purposed to give each of us the option to choose Him and avoid Hades as our final destination upon our death in Stage 2.

With this option in mind, let's explore the results of remaining in Stage 2 until your death. Several aspects of life will take place as one remains in this stage. One of the first is realizing you have no help from the Lord to make it less difficult. And, always remember that because you neglected salvation, your next location of existence will automatically become fatal.

STAGE 3

S tage 3 is a person that has lived on earth without Christ in their life. This personal choice will leave you in the same condition as the rich man in Luke, chapter 15. Harsh conditions and this new eternal location will immediately worsen, and your selected eternal destination will be realized. The hope for a better future in eternity will have expired. Your new existence will be void of any comfort, rest, or hope of ever being relieved from your present condition. Obtaining the peace of God will elude you entirely, and your future will always be bleak. You will spend eternity without the Lord, separated from God, and will spend your final existence in Eternal damnation — Hades!

The peace and hope previously made available will never be found, and the feelings of excitement will be reduced to the best you can do for yourself. As we rely on our emotions, feelings, and natural way of thinking, our existence will nearly be intolerable and certainly not enriched. This choice you've made will block any help from the Lord to live a life of greatest pleasure or accomplishments.

A good friend of mine explained it this way: *We each are made with a hole in our heart that can only be filled by the Lord.* Nothing else will satisfy this empty space within. And, there is only one way to satisfy this void in our soul, and that is the presence of the Holy Spirit.

I have thought about that for many years and see where this thinking may have more significance than I first thought. There always seems to be a void in those I encounter in life that do not know the Lord. Something is missing that always goes away when they come to the saving knowledge of Christ.

The opportunity to escape Eternal damnation is no longer available, so putting off making a choice in Stage 2 has been left to chance. Chances are your realization of this reality will come to mind, but now it's too late. Maybe like the rich man we discussed earlier.

In looking at Stage 3, Eternal damnation, from Scripture, several mental word pictures are given. The following excerpts from the bible are self-explanatory as they describe this location in eternity called Hades or Eternal damnation:

Matthew 5:22:
"You are in danger of the fires of hell."

Matthew 7:13:
"The highway to hell is broad, and its gate is wide for the many who choose that way."

Matthew 10:28:
"Fear only God, who can destroy both soul and body in hell."

Mark 9:43:
"It's better to enter eternal life with only one hand than to go into the unquenchable fires of hell with two hands."

Luke 16:24:
"The rich man shouted, 'Father Abraham, have pity! Send Lazarus over here to dip the tip of his finger in water and cool my tongue. I am in anguish in these flames.'"

2 Peter 2:4:
"For God did not spare even the angels who sinned. He threw them into hell, in gloomy pits of darkness, where they are being held until the day of judgment."

Revelation 20:14-15:
"Then death and the grave were thrown into the lake of fire. This lake of fire is the second death. And anyone whose name was not found recorded in the Book of Life was thrown into the lake of fire."

The above Scriptures give a clear picture of our destination after living in Stage 2 without accepting the option made available through Jesus Christ. When everything regarding our destination is left to chance — this is the end result!

Consider the Path you will Choose to Follow

> Matthew 7:13-14:
> *"You can enter God's Kingdom only through the narrow gate. The highway to hell is broad, and its gate is wide for the many who choose that way."*

The broad pathway consists of choosing your own way with no help from the Lord. Your choice to refuse the Lord is granted — as well as the results.

> *"But the gateway to life is very narrow and the road is difficult, and only a few ever find it."*

Few choose to deny their fleshly desires and call upon the Lord to follow after Him because what feels good and excites their passions is allowed to dominate their lives. In actuality, they are a slave to their own fleshly desires — sin.

> Luke 13:24:
> *"Work hard to enter the narrow door to God's Kingdom, for many will try to enter but will fail."*

Denying your fleshly desires is a decision, and with the Lords help, takes work but will yield your pathway to enter that narrow door. The path to wholeness and learning how these natural desires will led only to failure and damnation.

Why will they fail? Because there is only one way to enter, and we find Scripture in the bible that provides this answer as well:

John 14:6:
"Jesus told him, 'I am the way, the truth, and the life. No one can come to the Father except through me.'"

Philippians 3:9:
"And become one with him. I no longer count on my own righteousness through obeying the law; rather, I become righteous through faith in Christ. For God's way of making us right with himself depends on faith."

Getting our mind and thinking renewed and our actions in line with God's Word is crucial. Executing our faith in what He says will clear our path and avoid spiritual failure in our future.

God has given us the path to follow as described in the bible. Any other guidelines or religious beliefs or rituals that cause us to follow something other than the Truth found in the bible is fatal.

John 17:3;
"And this is the way to have eternal life—to know you, the only true God, and Jesus Christ, the one you sent to earth."

The Heart of God is Revealed in the Parable of the Lost Sheep

Luke 18:12-14:
"If a man has a hundred sheep and one of them wanders away, what will he do? Won't he leave the ninety-nine others on the hills and go out to search for the one that is lost? And if he finds it, I tell you the truth, he will rejoice over it more than over the ninety-nine that didn't wander away! In the same way, it is not my heavenly Father's will that even one of these little ones should perish."

God does not want any one to perish and suffer physical death before they receive salvation! He wants them to refrain from wandering off on their own only to be lost forever. He gave His Son as a sacrifice to pay the sin debt in full and give humankind a way to choose Heaven over Hades as their eternal destination.

Look carefully at some of the characteristics of Eternal damnation from Scripture. We see it brings to mind the constant unquenchable fire, the anguish of the flames always present. Mentioned also is the desire for something cool to drink, gloom and doom and darkness, existing without God's presence ever again, and the hopelessness of never being able to escape these conditions — ever!

Also, we learn from Scripture that Satan and his hoodlums (demons) will be present and who knows what havoc they will cause in their final location throughout eternity. And, those fallen angels that came with Satan when he was cast down to earth, are awaiting judgement in gloom and doom (Jude 1:6).

It looks like a most undesirable place to spend any time and certainly not eternity. And since, we can choose to avoid it — why not make a choice now and skip over this eternal destination and move on into Stage 4 where this will eliminate and secure any possibility of ending up in the _unquenchable fires of hell_?

Stage 3 is when we die in our sin and choose not to accept or believe in God's Son. This transfer from our physical body signifies that our Spirit and Soul will then live forever in our new spiritual dimension in eternity in bodies that will not die.

The physical body cannot take on a new spiritual existence because it isn't designed for eternity. Neither is our physical body capable of dying for our sin and satisfying God's requirement for sins penalty. Hence, that's why God sent Jesus to earth!

This leaves us only one choice to be redeemed from our sin nature, and that is in accepting Christ and believing by faith in what He had done. He died for a good reason and that was to free us from the sin nature we were born into.

Isn't that very clear from reading the Word? Knowing this fact gives us no excuse. Why? Because we can choose now and avoid Eternal damnation altogether!

Stage 3 is the final stage for a non-believer. Our birth ensures a sinful nature once we enter the world. Our birth places us in our current Stage 2 existence. If we choose to remain a nonbeliever, our presence keeps us in this state, and there is no hope for any other conclusion at life's end.

The only path for escape is offered by God and is available to each and every person born into the world during their lifetime. The same consequences are common to every human without favor or partiality.

We are born into the world a nonbeliever and have a God-given choice to step out from under that curse and be removed by faith into the belief realm that God has offered by just believing in Jesus Christ.

The problem is that humanity many times rejects God's offer of Salvation and does not receive his ticket to skip Stage 3 and move into Stage 4. This 'ticket' is presented in the following Scriptures:

The Good News

> Romans 1:16-17:
> *"For I am not ashamed of this Good News about Christ. It is the power of God at work, saving everyone who believes — the Jew first and also the Gentiles."*
>
> *"This Good News tells us how God makes us right in his sight. This is accomplished from start to finish by faith. As the Scriptures say. 'It is through faith that a righteous person has life.'"*

Scriptures tell us in Romans 1:18-32 that each person can see God's Presence in all that has been created. Our earth is full of His creative evidence for all to see and experience. All of the heavens and earth didn't just explode and came out of nowhere into existence. There was a great deal of creating done, and it is evident to all humanity.

To believe otherwise is willful denial of what is evident. Choosing to remain ignorant reveals our unwillingness to view things as they are as seen in our world today. Denying what is right in front and all around us is a personal choice, and we each are responsible for ourselves.

There are no excuses should we deny His creation. To reject these visible indicators is foolish. This kind of thinking opens a channel to developing an anti-God attitude, which is the opposite of what God desires. Choosing to put yourself in this way of thinking is contrary to the Truth expressed in God's Word and puts one in direct opposition against God.

This kind of thinking is a stronghold because it stands against what God has revealed in His Word. The results — Eternal damnation, and we enter Stage 3 by choice. Choosing not to believe is choosing certain Eternal damnation!

Free will has been allotted to each of us and allows us to accept God's solution to Passover Stage 3. Stage 3 <u>is not a desirable end</u> and should be avoided at all costs. Since God has provided a way for each to escape this eternal destination, the question arises — why wouldn't <u>everyone</u> choose to pass over Eternal damnation and remove themselves from everlasting doom?

God does not send anyone to Hades. How do we get there? We can choose to bypass this fiery destination by choosing His solution — His offer of Salvation. Being stubborn and resistant, like the many non-believing Israelites following Moses, will yield a difficult life on earth and Eternal damnation once you die.

Damnation is complete separation from God, forever, and that alone will be so miserable it's hard to imagine. Not to mention the unquenchable thirst, fiery atmosphere, darkness, demonic harassment, rancid smells, never-ending heat, and the inability to never escape, unable to die and get out, unable to find any relief and know that this Stage 3 will never end — remember, it's for eternity — forever.

Obviously, I have not been to this fiery grave, but I had what I called a mild, suggestive introduction to what it might be like. When flying into Vietnam at night, we were approaching the runway ready to land, and rockets were coming in to discourage our pilots, so they powered the engines up just before touching down, and we quickly reversed our downward direction back up again and out of the way. Quite a thrill I might add!

We circled the landing strip, and once cleared for landing, we proceed down to land the commercial aircraft on the runway. Once again, the rockets started coming in, and we zoomed up quickly to avoid any possible harm. I believe I also got to slightly sense the beginnings of what a G-force might feel like.

This time I thought for sure a wing-tip would hit the ground, but it did not, and we continued away from the exploding resistance that awaited us on the ground. It was a North Vietnamese resistance party trying to let us know that we weren't welcome. I really thought they could have given the same message another way, but no one ask me beforehand because I would have gladly offered a much better welcome than that.

I'm not sure how long it was before our third attempt, but my buddy and I said to each other — 'That's not the welcoming committee I was expecting upon arrival. Do you think we'll make it to the ground alive?'

The third approach went as planned, and we safely landed on the ground where other Marines were waiting to pick us up. When we got to the exit door of the plane, I stopped in almost shock and turned to my buddy and said — *This must be what hell is like when you first enter.*

The extreme night heat, the rotten smells of burnt surrounds, and death, the eerie fiery lighting made the whole humid atmosphere suffocating and uninviting to enter. We had already been stationed in Okinawa for a year and thought the heat would not be so noticeable. Wrong!

As a result of that experience, I've always wondered if this was my glimpse of what Eternal damnation might be like. I immediately knew I did not want any part of it. Eternity in an atmosphere like that would depress even Mother Teresa.

Another Scripture that brought Alarm to my Spirit

> John 8:44:
> *"For you are children of your father the devil, and you love to do the evil things he does. He was a murderer from the beginning. He has always hated the truth in him. When he lies, it is consistent with his character; for he is a liar and the father of lies."*

The Bad News

So, practicing things in opposition to Scripture are lies of the devil and classified as strongholds. Doing life in direct resistance to God's ways are strongholds of opposition that reject any Scriptural application. So, beliefs contrary to Scripture, are lies, opposition, and strongholds against the bible.

These strongholds of lies have consequences and practicing them places us in collaboration with the devil, Satan, the father of lies! Wrong choice, wrong team, wrong path to follow, and certainly the wrong results when all is finalized.

I don't want to be in business with the devil or help him in any way. Therefore, I chose to follow after the Lord and learn how to conduct myself so that I'm not following after the father of lies — Satan. His part in life is evident both from Scripture and in reality.

We already know the devil is doomed and where he will spend eternity. Forget that. I'll choose my option and spend eternity with the Lord instead. That's an easy choice and one I've gladly made.

Our Passover Today

Christ came to earth many years after the Fall of humanity in the Garden of Eden, providing a means to move from Stage 2, avoiding Stage 3, and on to the next stage. This is based on what Christ had done by sacrificing Himself on the cross and satisfying God's penalty for sin that we received at birth.

The suffering of Jesus on the cross provided many benefits that can be enjoyed — both now and in our future. His sacrifice, choosing death so we could be redeemed, is only one of many benefits He made available. The bible is full of promises and principles and ways to combat both our current physical and spiritual environment.

His choice to make available these many blessings was to make available an assurance our existence could be more enjoyable and secure as we leaned on Him to show us a better way. Besides, He already knew our weaknesses, and the cross made us acceptable to God and released The Father to assist us as we journey through life so we can live victoriously.

Remember, in the Old Testament, when God put a plague on the land of Egypt and sent the death angel to kill the first born in each household? This plague also included the first born male animals that belonged to the Egyptians (Exodus 12:12). This plague was to let Pharaoh know that God was in control, and Pharaoh had no way to combat against Him.

This was a judgment from God executed against all gods in Egypt to let Pharaoh experience His wrath. This exhibit of His almighty power was experienced when God's wrath was implemented. This action was to prove who the real God was without question. But, God had a way out for the Israelites that were enslaved to the Pharaoh and living as their slaves.

God intentionally provided a way out for the Israelites, so they would not suffer His wrath of death on their firstborn. He provided instructions to follow and provided a means to escape the death angel that was soon coming.

He instructed them to place blood over their doorposts as a sign for the death angel to *pass over* that home where the blood was place (Exodus 12:23). This is referred to as Passover (also called Festival of Unleavened Bread) (Luke 22:1) and has been celebrated ever since that time.

Our Passover today is our accepting Christ into our lives and allowing His shed Blood as our covering, so our death is not into Hades or Eternal damnation. We are saved from this permanent separation from God and can avoid the punishment for our sins and receive life with God, now, and forever.

We are given a way to *passover* the penalty of sin and escape the death intended for all who deny God's Son and carry on without Him. It is a fatal end to a life on earth, which the Lord did not want us to choose or experience.

By accepting Christ, we formalize and receive His suffering on the cross as payment for our sin. By doing this, we accept the shedding of His Blood as a covering over our lives. We are then receiving Him as our Passover Lamb, and will skip Stage 3 (Eternal damnation) and move directly into Stage 4. Saved by Christ, knowing our physical death will only bring with it eternity in Heaven instead.

Scripture relates that each person will die twice. So, what is the first death? Let's look at a nonbeliever and see what the bible says.

Our First and Second Death as a Nonbeliever

Our first death is our physical dying, where we will be found without the Lord as our savior at life's end. Then the second death will be our Spiritual Death. This second death will occur as the goats, and the sheep are determined at the judgement seat (Matthew 5:22) when we stand before the Lord.

For those who did not choose the Lord during their physical life, they will be separated from the believers. This separation will cause them to be sent to the lake of fire, where they will spend their eternity apart from God.

This is the Eternal damnation they deserve because their sin nature was never redeemed and they must suffer for their sin. Why this destination? It is because they did not accept Christs's Death on the cross for themselves and receive God's offered redemption.

Our First and Second Death as a Believer

Unlike the nonbeliever, when we accept Christs's Death on the cross before we physically die, it becomes our first Death — *death to self* (where we choose to follow the Lord rather than our natural instincts and reasoning). Then, when we physically die, it is counted as our second death, and eternity will be spent with the Lord forever because we accepted Christ as our Passover Lamb (1 Corinthians 5:7) while in Stage 2.

We will be the *sheep* (the believers) that are separated from the *goats* (the nonbeliever) at the judgement seat. The Lord will determine who knew (ginosko = personal relationship) Him, and He will determine those who only knew (onida = had heard of only) about Him.

In summary, each human being is appointed to die twice. The believer applies the Blood of Christ over himself (first death) by faith, so the second death will not send him to Eternal damnation/Hades (Revelation 20:6). The first death is to self (share in the first resurrection from His death on the cross with Christ). And the second death will be our physical death. An excellent choice — right?

Check out Scripture on this Subject

> 1 Corinthians 15:20-23:
> *"But in fact, Christ has been raised from the dead. He is the first of a great harvest of all who have died. So you see, just as death came into the world through a man (Adam), now the resurrection from the dead has begun through another man (Christ)."*
>
> *"Just as everyone dies because we all belong to Adam, everyone who belongs to Christ will be given new life. But there is an order to this resurrection: Christ was raised as the first of the harvest; then all who belong to Christ will be raised when he comes back."*
>
> Revelation 21:8:
> *"But the cowardly, the unbelieving, the vile, the murderers, the sexually immoral, those who practice*

magic arts, the idolaters and all liars—they will be consigned to the fiery lake of burning sulfur. This is the second death."

Check out Scripture and see how God works out our Forgiveness from Sin

"The Scriptures tell us, 'The first man, Adam, became a living person.' But the last Adam—that is, Christ—is a <u>life-giving Spirit</u>."

"What comes first is the natural body, then the spiritual body comes later."

"Adam, the first man, was made from the dust of the earth, while Christ, the second man, came from heaven."

"Earthly people are like the earthly man, and heavenly people are like the heavenly man."

"Just as we are now like the earthly man, we will someday be like the heavenly man."

"What I am saying, dear brothers and sisters, is that our physical bodies cannot inherit the Kingdom of God. These dying bodies cannot inherit what will last forever."

"But let me reveal to you a wonderful secret. We will not all die, but we will all be transformed!"

"It will happen in a moment, in the blink of an eye, when the last trumpet is blown. For when the trumpet sounds, those who have died will be raised to live forever. And we who are living will also be transformed."

"For our dying bodies must be transformed into bodies that will never die; our mortal bodies must be transformed into immortal bodies."

"Then, when our dying bodies have been transformed into bodies that will never die, this Scripture will be fulfilled."

"Death is swallowed up in victory.
O death, where is your victory?
O death, where is your sting?"

"For sin is the sting that results in death, and the
law gives sin its power."
"But thank God! He gives us victory over sin and
death through our Lord Jesus Christ."
"So, my dear brothers and sisters, be strong and
immovable. Always work enthusiastically for the Lord,
for you know that nothing you do for the Lord is ever
useless."

Then, I read in the Book of Revelation that Death and the Grave are eliminated from existence, meaning their removal signifies we live forever and will never die again. This never dying again means our choice for eternity will go on forever.

You can't die once you reach eternity — Death doesn't exist anymore. What a thought that is!

What is Circumcision Anyway?

In the Old Testament, circumcision was representative of the Israelites acting in obedience to God. This placed them outwardly in submission to God by the cutting away of their flesh. A symbolic symbol of their condition before God.

All male foreigners wanting to participate in the Passover with the native-born Israelites were required to be circumcised in order to celebrate this special event. If they were not circumcised they were not to participate. No uncircumcised male was to eat the Passover meal (Exodus 12:28). This was the law at that time in history.

What is circumcision? It was the cutting away of flesh to signify a marking and action taken in obedience to God. When Moses hesitated to follow through and act in obedience, he was offered death from God for lack of compliance. His hesitation almost cost him his life — it was that important to God and represented obedience.

What does this have to do with anything today? Scripture tells us what the significance of circumcision is in our culture today. This biblical reference is found in:

Romans 2:29:
"No, a true Jew is one whose heart is right with God. And true circumcision is not merely obey the letter of the law; rather, it is a change of heart produced by God's Spirit. And a person with a changed heart seeks praise from God, not from people."

Romans 2:25:
"The Jewish ceremony of circumcision has value only if you obey God's law. But if you don't obey God's law, you are no better off than an uncircumcised Gentile."

Wait a minute! What is being said in Scripture? This is confusing. Read on in Romans 2:28 which reads:
"For you are not a true Jew just because you were born of Jewish parents or because you have gone through the ceremony of circumcision."

Old Testament Fact: The Jewish faith came from the law that required a person to be circumcised, showing his obedience to the law, or else, a person could not belong to the family of God.

Looking closer at Ephesians chapter 2, we get a picture of how the Jews believed, in their natural understanding, and how they viewed those outside their culture.

Ephesians 2:11:
"Don't forget that you Gentiles used to be outsiders. You're called "uncircumcised heathens" by the Jews, who were proud of their circumcision, even though it affected only their bodies and not their hearts."

This means for the believer today that God wants to deal with our hearts. Being circumcised in the flesh does not carry the same meaning as the law because of the coming of Christ.

Scripture Sums it up Well

> Galatians 5:1-4:
> *"So Christ has truly set us free. Now make sure that you stay free, and don't get tied up again in slavery to the law."*
>
> *"Listen! I, Paul, tell you this: If you are counting on circumcision to make you right with God, then Christ will be of no benefit to you."*
>
> *"I'll say it again. If you are trying to find favor with God by being circumcised, you must obey every regulation in the whole law of Moses."*

If you are trying to make yourselves right with God by keeping the law, you have been cut off from Christ! You have fallen away from God's grace and are acting out the separation by fleshly means rather than by the changing of your heart! And, as we just read in Romans 2:29 — this effort is worthless in the eyes of God.

The Old Testament application of the law has been replaced by the New Testament application of grace and faith in Jesus Christ. The law, which we could not live in obedience to, revealed that humanity could not fulfill the law, so God's grace purposely replaced it, and we now have the ability by faith to fulfill all the law of old by our faith in Christ. How again? Because of what Christ has accomplished by satisfying God penalty for sin by dying on the cross.

Fleshly efforts have been replace by — believing by faith and receive what God made accessible just by our believing in Christ and accepting His accomplishments in our place. By faith we offer up a sacrificial lamb, Christ, like in the Old Testament, which covers our sin, according to God.

Accepting the fact of Christ and receiving His death, His burial, and Resurrection and all it provides gives each of us our passage back to the Father. No more enmity between God and man because of sin. The curse that had been placed on us before we were born into the world has been removed.

Now, we can be reborn — *born again* — and removed from under the curse initiated by Adam and Eve's sin that we were born into at our physical birth into the world.

Look Further into Scripture and Learn

> Colossians 2:11:
> *"When you came to Christ, you were 'circumcised,' but not by a physical procedure. Christ performed a spiritual circumcision — the cutting away of your sinful nature."*

So, looking at the physical circumcision of the flesh as a way to get salvation is a lie of the devil he wants you to believe. But, the truth awaits our viewing as we read on in Scripture.

> John 17:3:
> *"And this is the way to have eternal life—to know you, the only true God, and Jesus Christ, the one you sent to earth."*

> Galatians 5:2:
> *"Listen! I, Paul, tell you this: If you are counting on circumcision to make you right with God, then Christ will be of no benefit to you."*

> Titus 1:10:
> *"For there are many rebellious people who engage in useless talk and deceive others. This is especially true of those who insist on circumcision for salvation."*

Wow! That reveals a lot about the many religions available today. This one area of thinking can be found everywhere today from those who preach a different gospel. The only true gospel will focus on Jesus Christ and what He has accomplished on the cross in obedience to God the Father.

Thinking a ritual or ceremony will save us is futile regarding salvation. Believing anything other than the Holy Bible is false teaching with a little truth woven throughout. It has the appearance of a saving religion or that a little different salvation package exists. There is not Salvation apart from Christ! Salvation is not available but only through Jesus Christ!

Scripture tells us point blank how to get to God the Father and how things work. And it tells us plainly in the Book of John with the following:

> John 14:6:
> *"Jesus told him, 'I am the way, the truth, and the life. No one can come to the Father except through me.'"*

Other Scripture providing a Colorful picture of Christ and the Reason for His Coming

> Galatians 1:4:
> *"Jesus gave his life for our sins, just as God our Father planned, in order to rescue us from this evil world in which we live."*

> Ephesians 2:18:
> *"Now all of us can come to the Father through the same Holy Spirit because of what Christ has done for us."*

> Hebrews 1:5:
> *"For God never said to any angel what he said to Jesus: 'You are my Son, Today I have become your Father,' God also said, 'I will be his Father, and he will be my Son.'"*

1 Peter 1:3-7:

"All praise to God, the Father of our Lord Jesus Christ. It is by his great mercy that we have been born again, because God raised Jesus Christ from the dead. Now we live with great expectations,"

"And we have a priceless inheritance—an inheritance that is kept in heaven for you, pure and undefiled, beyond the reach of change and decay."

"And through your faith, God is protecting you by his power until you receive this salvation, which is ready to be revealed on the last day for all to see."

"So be truly glad. There is wonderful joy ahead, even through you have to endure many trials for a little while."

"These trials will show that your faith is genuine. It is being tested as fire tests and purifies gold—though your faith is far more precious than mere gold. So when your faith remains strong through many trials, it will bring you much praise and glory and honor on the day when Jesus Christ is revealed to the whole world."

It's amazing! Think a believer has glory days ahead or what? Our life is a lot more brief than you may think. We are just passing through and then on to eternity. Our temporary life on earth provides the opportunity to receive God's grace. His provisions will take us all the way past Eternal damnation (Stage 3) and all the way to Heaven (Stage 7). Don't you see that eternity can be selected NOW and that it is our choice and our choice only.

All that awaits is your acceptance of God's way and choosing to receive by believing in Jesus Christ! This isn't rocket science, folks! Even I could understand this offer, even the fine print (there isn't any). The bible declares what is available and what to do to receive Christ, which includes Heaven as our eternal destination! Plain and simple!

For your own sake, choose life. How about making today as your date to select this opportunity before it expires. The time of closure is imminent. What if there isn't another opportunity? You know that when you take your last breath (you expire) the offer expires as well? If you're tired of being preached to why not choose the offer and see for yourself?

If you do, you'll become the one preaching to others and driving them crazy. Even that has been fun for me because I procrastinated at the full offer. After all, I had no intension of yielding to something I could not see, meet or feel, or talk to. It was pure nonsense and I didn't want anything not real to me, supposedly running my life. I didn't want others calling me crazy because I was believing in something not real — not even tangible.

It really is a lot more fun on the other side (choosing to be a believer) because much is revealed by the Holy Spirit as you journey through life with the Lord. You'll realize that He, the Holy Spirit, is on a frequency you didn't know existed before this decision to accept His Salvation Package, and the Holy Spirit was implanted in you.

Get with the program and receive God's Passover option and remove yourself from experiencing Stage 3. This Passover option is all that's needed to crossover to the other side with no sin baggage or penalties or fear of damnation. It's an option that will last way beyond this lifetime that you will be extremely glad you made before your short time on earth ends. He's waiting right now so you don't have to!

As discussed at the beginning of this chapters, after you make your choice and accept Christ — this places you in Stage 4.

The difference from Stage 2 is that now you have accepted God's offer of Salvation; it allows the Lord to change our status with God and for us to be transformed into a Believer starting our new life in Christ.

What did Christ do to Make this Stage Available?

Read the following Scripture to illuminate God's option:

> Ephesians 4:14:
> *"Then we will no longer be immature like children.*
> *We won't be tossed and blown about by every wind of*

new teaching. We will not be influenced when people try to trick us with lies so clever they sound like the truth."

What? *"...lies so clever they sound like the truth."* This could be describing what we hear today. Yes, that is exactly correct. Cleverly spoken words that really sound like the truth but are not. Our selection of who we listen to is woven together with our natural thinking and can causes us great delusion. It can cause lies to be understood as truth. This will leads us away from the Truth of God's Word.

That is why it is so important for each of us to read the Word of God and call upon the Holy Spirit to help us understand what we are reading from the bible. His Word enlightens our understanding and gives us cause to question what we allow in our minds. His Spirit gives us hearing that is inspired by Him and a voice of Truth in which to listen.

Since we always have a choice, we need the Lord's help to decipher what we hear and read. So, we choose to either listen with our natural thinking, believing there is no other (a lie) and apply this reasoning into our lives or, choose to line up what we've heard or read in Scripture.

To believe with our thinking (without God's help) is very common but brings us back to the question — Who do you want to believe? A serious question with very different results. Should we continue our ways before we accepted the Lord and believe what the world tells us? Or, do we take what we hear and read and measure it against the principles and truths we find in the bible?

What the world relies on is straight from the devil, the father of lies. Or — do we check out his lies with the Truth of God? Choosing to test what we hear against what the Lord tells us will reveal a much-needed reason to thoroughly check things out. Our comparing a lie with a truth from Scripture will clarify the source of much worldly information.

Look at What the Bible tells us Regarding our Mind

Romans 7:23:
"But there is another power within me that is at war with my mind. This power makes me a slave to the sin that is still within me."

Romans 8:6:
"Thank God! The answer is in Jesus Christ our Lord. So you see how it is. In my mind I really want to obey God's law, but because of my sinful nature I am a slave to sin."

The power of the Holy Spirit that now resides within me as a believer will provide the strength I need to break free from the bondage of sin (Romans 7:24). This power was made available when we accepted the Lord Jesus Christ into our hearts and follow His leading!

Coming out from under the sin burden opens us up to receive truth and wisdom from God that was not available prior to our conversion. That choice we made to accept Christ has opened up our channel directly with God. This open channel gives us godly direction and removes the enmity once caused by sin.

Listening as we Journey

How does one listen to the truth rather than lies? The answer is quite simple. We learn wisdom from reading the Word of God — the Bible. If you don't like this approach please be aware wisdom comes from no where else! Obtaining knowledge is not the same as wisdom. We must be saved and willing to grow up, and proceed with an open mind, and renew our minds, and learn for ourselves.

Listening to God is not hearing and believing all the voices around you, but listening specifically to God's Word. It has been written for this very purpose and will teach us how to listen to God and how to turn away from satanic clamor and worldly ideas that hits us from every angle every day.

Voices we hear everyday come in many sources. Consider the following as sources that will come into your mind. Suggestive notions of thought filled fancies, getting our way without any consequences with no regards for others. Maybe doing to others anything to fulfill a desire within, or getting even with someone that's brought you harm. It could be believing God wouldn't send you to an Eternal damnation, contemplating unrealistic goals of grandeur, discerning through evil spirits whispering in your ear, and acting out your wrong worldly thinking rather than follow Scripture.

All voices are not of the Lord. Comparing what your hear with Scripture will help in separating them. All are clamor if they are contrary to the Word of God. We must learn the source of these voices and discern which to listen and which to avoid. It is critical to hear the voice of God, above this clamor and it takes practice to hear better!

If our vision is clouded with ungodly eyesight, we will miss the Truth of God in almost everything we do. Of course, being spiritually blind, not believing there is a better way to do life is commonly surmised. Knowing these possibilities should cause us to proceed with caution.

Figuring the source is essential. If you think that what you don't know won't hurt you is very dangerous. Believing you've figured out life and how to live it in survival mode is a struggle at best. Taking advice from those with your same thinking and believing the same approach is scriptural needs confirmation. And, confirming your decision based on these sources, rather than God's truth, is totally misguided.

Believing the church is lame and needs to develop some gumption, and deal with this believing in God stuff because it is phony nonsense is most certainly a lie. Basing our thinking and decisions on watching someone that goes to church, but doesn't possess any godly characteristics you want is dangerous. Remember, some worldly believers don't always allow the Lord to change their character and choose to continue on doing what they were doing before accepting Christ.

You may be eliminating God completely because you see no evidence or benefit from wasting your time and money on anything this misleading or unrealistic. Be wise, and check things out for clarity, and be certain with facts before you excuse what's real and what is the Truth. Ensure you have not fallen for a lie that will send you to eternal damnation!

Protecting ourselves from people that might hurt us is common and very understandable. Our survival instinct is built-in and has a purpose. Its purpose can also be misused. Its purpose can better be understood from a spiritual set of eyes that can see past our limited blind physical eyesight. Thinking there is nothing than the physical realm we live is also a lie of the devil. Read Ephesians, chapter 6, and think about what it has to say.

There is much more to see than our natural eyes can visualize. There is also a spiritual world all around us and we must utilize our spiritual eyes in order to see and deal with its existence. We remain spiritually blind until we accept Christ. Then, we have the ability to see with our spiritual eyes and steadily become aware of much more than our physical eyes can see.

We so easily believe only our experiences, feelings, and what our emotions conjure up, which places us in the wrong mode of thinking. We have no ability to deal with the demonic spiritual world and all it brings our way. And, not believing it's in existence only keeps us contained in the physical realm alone without any spiritual capabilities to combat the forces of evil existing where we live.

Accepting this Godless form of existence leaves us in Stage 2 with only the possibility of Stage 3 as our eternal destiny. Refusing the Lord's option of salvation that's available is mere existence and not a very good one at that.

Those Israelites traveling through the desert is a view of reality when you don't believe in God and have His Presence all around you.

This kind of living, without faith, leaves no room to believe anything God has to offer or how He wants us to live. It's like running a race with no sense of how the course is laid out, which way to run, and having one-leg tied to the other.

Receiving Christ, being *born again*, removes us from any possibility of ending in Stage 3. You are put in right standing with God the Father because of the sacrifice Jesus provided by dying in our place and making a way to be received into God's Family.

Being *born again* causes your name to be written in the Lambs Book of Life and the heavenly roster is an extremely special place for your name to be written. When Christ returns, this book will be opened, and all those names that have been written in it will receive their reward and spend eternity with the Lord (Revelation 21:27).

Consider your options carefully. The following Scriptures reveal the way to avoid Hades or Eternal damnation. Read and consider the choices that lead the way to everlasting life:

Mark 16:16:
"Anyone who believes and is baptized will be saved. But anyone who refuses to believe will be condemned."

John 3:3:
Jesus replied *"I tell you the truth, unless you are bored again, you cannot see the Kingdom of God."*

John 3:18:
"There is no judgment against anyone who believes in him. But anyone who does not believe in him has already been judged for not believing in God's one and only Son."

John 5:24:
"I tell you the truth, those who listen to my message and believe in God who sent me have eternal life. They

will never be condemned for their sins, but they have already passed from death into life."

Romans 10:4:
"For Christ has already accomplished the purpose for which the law was given. As a result, all who believe in him are made right with God."

Romans 10:9:
"If you confess with your mouth that Jesus is Lord and believe in your heart that God raised him from the dead, you will be saved."

1 Timothy 1:15:
"This is a trustworthy saying, and everyone should accept it: 'Christ Jesus came into the world to save sinners—and I am the worst of them all.'"

James 1:21:
"So get rid of all the filth and evil in your lives, and humbly accept the word God has planted in your hearts, for it has the power to save your souls."

1 John 5:13:
"I have written this to you who believe in the name of the Son of God, so that you may know you have eternal life."

These excerpts from the bible tell a story that needs to be read and followed. This decision opens the only entrance to Heaven. It's a freebie that cost one decision and made by faith.

Following these Truths from Scripture can eliminate the possibility of entering Stage 3 and spending eternity there. These Scriptures provide the hope and path to better living and spending Eternity with our Creator — God!

P.S. The previous two chapters are what I call <u>Preacher Print</u>. This involves repeated wording to stress the urgency and necessity to understand the message. And, in the understanding, to point out the action required by each person to save their soul from Hell. The message is presented using a variety of descriptions in numerous paragraphs saying the same thing.

Unlike a sermon, you are given a message in print and the voice you hear is your own. It is that voice in your mind that verbalizes quietly what you just read. Remember, this is one of those voices you hear everyday. It is a voice you listen to, reason with, and are in direct visitation with — yourself. Sometimes, this voice can provide wrong conclusions should it not be knowledgeable enough to give good godly advice.

This is why renewing your mind from Scriptures is extremely important, because it will change your way of thinking and align your thoughts with the Truth of God. This information has been sent from God, directly to humanity, with instructions that can save us from the curse we must overcome.

And, with His help, we can live in the Promised Land and receive a blessed life and benefit from all His many gifts and blessings!

❧

CHAPTER FOUR

Now that I'm Saved — What's Next?

Accepting the Lord into your life is so simple. Sometimes we make it difficult because we think we have to do more than just pray to receive our salvation. But, this simple acceptance of Christ begins your Spiritual Birth.

You will begin to experience a sensitivity to *things* around you that were never before seen or realized. Your Spirit will come alive inside of you and provide insight never before thought possible or knew existed. New feelings and awareness come alive on the inside as you relate to the spiritual newest around you.

A New Awareness Will Come Alive in You

The Holy Spirit of God will take up residence within you, and provide promptings and guidance. This new *spiritual birth* will cause your own spirit to come alive and be receptive to new information, accelerated understanding, a level of discernment, and an awareness that was not previously present in your life.

Reading the bible will take on a new dimension as well, and your new understanding will start to kick in, and you will begin to increase in knowledge and to gather wisdom only God can provide. This new realm of existence will bring the wisdom needed to live a better life.

Your spirit will recognize that a spiritual world is in existence all around you. You will learn that evil functions under the guidance of the devil, and you will become alerted to its presence. The Holy Spirit that now dwells inside you will stir your spirit, revealing new activity, and bring a new awareness to your surroundings.

Scripture will begin to come alive as you read from the bible. Your understanding will increase as you listen and hear with new eyes and ears. You will start to hear and see with new receptive senses that will assist you in your walk with the Lord.

Seeing and understanding that the world you live in has much more depth than you first imagined. Your prior life without this *new sensitivity* will take on a different perspective as you reflect back. Amazingly, you will experience and discover your thinking will expand and grasp the world you live in with new ideas, wisdom, and understanding unheard of before.

Your spiritual vision will provide you with a sensitivity never before known about — maybe never before entered your mind. God is real, and your love for Him will take on a whole new understanding bringing comfort, insight, awareness, and a new feeling of peace and joy on the inside.

What Causes this to Happen?

You have now switched fathers. Satan no longer has power over you that drew your attention away from the Lord. Your desire to experience good will well up inside and turn your attention to new activities. God is in charge of everything you encounter, and your cooperation is essential to rule over the spiritual domain where you live. Your Father, God, has provided many principles and spiritual armor needed to overcome the evil forces in this world.

Your new Father, God, has adopted you into His family and written your name in the Book of Life that will be opened on Judgment Day. As you stand before God, your name will place you with the sheep (saved) and not with the goats (unsaved).

Your spiritual birth will enhance your reading of the bible, God's Word, and applying its principles will expand your individual life. His help and input will prove to lighten the journey and provide wisdom beyond your current understanding or imagination. Applying His principles will empower you to rise above many worldly challenges you will face in your present circumstances, both now and in the future.

Those are several of the significant provisions given to believers as they are applied to our lives. There is another side to this experience, and many will follow that will bless you. God showers us during our lifetime as we learn to receive all that God has provided. There is a great deal more to Salvation that's possible. These opportunities are available by the choices we make everyday. Remain vigilant and protect yourself — Don't fall back into your worldly thinking, and become unwilling to step out in faith and act on God's Word.

What is Faith?

Faith is believing that God will bring to pass what His Word says before it is a reality that you can see. The bible gives us a mental picture of what it is.

> Hebrews 11:1:
> *"Faith is the confidence that what we hope for will actually happen; it gives us assurance about things we cannot see."*

> Hebrews 11:6:
> *"And it is impossible to please God without faith. Anyone who wants to come to him must believe that God exists and that he rewards those who sincerely seek him."*

Reading in Hebrews chapter 11 reveals many bible characters who lived by faith and provide us today with examples of what was accomplished because they believed. Because they stood firm in their faith and helped change the world. Please read their stories for yourself.

Stage 4 of life can either be right on target, following God's leading, or it can leave you to yourself. Your choices are two-fold because you can live your life by faith or not. You can struggle on your own trying to accomplish in life what only God can do. You are saved but continue to rely on your worldly thinking and reasoning rather than venture out in faith and see what the bible provides to enhance your journey.

If we will dive into God's Word and start putting His written Word into practice, that will provide direction from the Holy Spirit to empower us forward. Our part is to learn and grow in obedience to God's Word and put it into action in our life by faith. That is believing what God has written and pursue the manifestation.

Without action on our part, God is not released to materialize His results in our life. God has His part, and we have ours. What we are expected to do will not be done by God. Sitting at home, waiting on a job, will most likely yield no godly results.

Our stepping out into the job market will provide God the opportunity to work in you life. *Stationary living will not yield action results.* God just doesn't operate that way. Learning what you can do, reacting to God's Word, will release Him to do His part.

It is the stepping out of where you are, and acting out what the bible instructs, and stop trying to accomplish and overpower circumstances by yourself. Not using the principles proposed in the bible to conquer that same problem is futile.

The bible is very clear to tell us that without Him, we will accomplish nothing (John 15:5). But, with His guidance and applied principles, we are able to do all things because of Christ living in us. And, He will work it all out for our good [Romans 8:28].

Stage 4 can be compared to the Israelites that went on with the

Lord as He led them out of Egypt (slavery). They accepted His offer to be freed from slavery, and willfully followed Him by faith. God had prepared a particular destination for them called the Promised Land.

As long as they followed His leading, they would reach their promised destination and receive all that God had intended to bless them. If they tried the journey under their own strength — life would remain difficult with no realized Promise at the end of their journey.

So, when they became disobedient and declined His leadership, they failed to receive what God intended and remained in the desert, struggling with their conditions until they died. Their 11-day journey turned into 40-years of continued failure, because of their unbelief. They were always on the move but never getting anywhere. When life was over, they could spend eternity with the Lord, but what a hard way to live life on earth.

Look at Scripture and see What God has Planned for Us

> Ephesians 2:8-9:
> *"God saved you by his grace when you believed. And you can't take credit for this; it is a gift from God. Salvation is not a reward for the good things we have done, so none of us can boast about it. For we are God's masterpiece. He has created us anew in Christ Jesus, so we can do the good things he planned for us long ago."*

What does this mean? It means we seriously consider what will happens, when we choose to following after the Lord or not? It means that before creation took place, God had a plan for us all. It means that His grace was freely given to become a new creation in Christ and that we have opportunity to live our lives in peace as we rest in our faith in Him.

The Israelites existence could have been so much better had they continued in faith in God rather than living life refusing to follow His leading. And, because they chose to go their own direction, they became lost and never obtained the peace of God, which was a part of their original intended destiny. Not to mention, they never received what God had waiting for them!

Faith in God could have taken them on a journey that led to a much better life and provided them with the many gifts, plenty, homes, productive crops from which to eat, assured victory as they battled their enemies, and a comfortable life when compared to the desert. Their destiny was undoubtedly a great opportunity that awaited them if they would have chosen to follow His instructions.

This experience was to teach them that they would struggle on their own, but with His help, they could overcome any obstacle. This message is relevant today. This example from the Old Testament is provided for us to learn from and choose a better way — obedience!

Check out What the Bible says about the Unbelieving Israelites

1 Corinthians 10:1-11:
"I don't want you to forget, dear brothers and sisters, about our ancestors in the wilderness long ago. All of them were guided by a cloud that moved ahead of them, and all of them walked through the sea on dry ground."

"In the cloud and in the sea, all of them were baptized as followers of Moses. All of them ate the same spiritual food, and all of them drank the same spiritual water. For they drank from the spiritual rock that traveled with them, and that rock was Christ."

"Yet, God was not pleased with most of them, and their bodies were scattered in the wilderness. These things happened as a warning to us, so that we would not crave evil things as they did or worship idols as some of them did."

"As the Scriptures say, 'the people celebrated with feasting and drinking, and they indulged in pagan

revelry. And we must not engage in sexual immorality as some of them did, causing 23,000 of them to die in one day."'

"Nor should we put Christ to the test, as some of them did and then died from snakebites. And don't grumble as some of them did, and then were destroyed by the angel of death."

"These things happened to them as an example for us. They were written down to warn us who live at the end of the age."

The Promised Land was made available to them all and was a location intended for them to prosper and live life to the fullest. The Lord wants all believers to enjoy life, and when we arrive at death's door, we will then pass from our physical life here into eternal life with God — forever!

This would be life at its very best. If humankind would cooperate with the process of learning God's way, every new day would be very exciting. A venture in faith provided by our God is fulfilling and accomplishes His plan for each of us. Talk about peace on earth!

Should we choose not to cooperate with God, then we will remain saved from Eternal damnation, but subject to the more difficult path as we journey along through living our life on the earth? A choice to not cooperate causes us to never experience God's best.

Stop wasting your time walking in disobedience and choose to continue with the Lord. There is much more to life than being saved. Really? Yes, there is a tremendous amount of blessing in following His leadership. We have open to us a God that knows our conditions and has prepared a way to conquer the kind of life the desert provides.

Since faith is the only way to please God — why not get with the program? Stop choosing to think your way through life and grasp the benefits made available from Scripture. It's readily available, but we do have to make some effort to get God's Word inside of us. He doesn't just pour His wisdom into us by force. But, He did provide a Book of Wisdom (the bible) to show us how to have the best life offers.

The Lord even provided the Holy Spirit to guide and assist us because He knew we could not do life independently and be blessed. We each have a choice, and desert living can be avoided. The Lord has so much planned for each of us, but we need to learn how to follow Him. We need to learn to practice what the bible teaches to capitalize on His many promises!

As we read in 1 Corinthians 10:1-10, this was a test for the Israelites to see how life is without God so they would choose His leading. It was their opportunity to act in obedience and reach the Promised Land *filled with milk and honey.*

According to their natural thinking, failing the test and pursuing life left the Israelites going in circles for 40-years rather than complete the journey in the intended 11-days. Are people really that stubborn? So it seems. Check out additional Scripture regarding choices and what to expect:

> Deuteronomy 8:1-3:
> *"Be careful to obey the commands I am giving you today. Then you will live and multiply, and you will enter and occupy the land the LORD swore to give your ancestors."*
>
> *"Remember how the LORD your God led you through the wilderness for these forty years, humbling you and testing you to prove your character, and to find out whether or not you would obey his commands."*
>
> *"Yes, he humbled you by letting you go hungry and then feeding you with manna, a food previously unknown to you and your ancestors. He did it to teach you that people do not live by bread alone; rather, we live by every word that comes from the mouth of the LORD."*

This is only the first three verses of Deuteronomy chapter 8. This is the Old Testament but has excellent practical validity today. We are given God's Word to help us gather His wisdom and understanding, so we will learn from others' mistakes and prosper.

Since God never changes, we can see His wisdom woven throughout the entire bible. This wisdom isn't old and outdated. These words have supernatural wisdom even for today.

We haven't outgrown His wisdom, nor have we proceeded in time to not benefit from its message of truth and godly power. Why can't we learn and accept His written word of instructions, and progress and grow-up in His wisdom? Life could be so much better!

Does our Pride get in the Way?

Pride is a relentless enemy that reveals its ugly head at every opportunity. Pride is a force we must guard against and be aware of its subtle influence. The bible gives many occasions where pride was responsible for outward actions that brought regret.

- The reason Adam and Eve wanted to become like God (Genesis 3:5).
- Why did King Saul resent David and tried to kill him (1 Samuel 1:18)?
- Was pride why King Hezekiah revealed his nations wealth to an enemy nation (Isaiah 39:2)?
- Pride was the reason why the disciples argued over rank in the coming kingdom of Christ (Luke 9:46).
- Didn't Joseph's brothers sell him into slavery because of their pride (Genesis 37:8)?
- Why did the Pharisees' resent Jesus and have such anger toward Him?
- Is it pride that causes people to continue in sin and avoid Christianity?

- Did you choose not to forgive someone who offended you because of your pride?
- Pride can cause you to reject asking forgiveness for your offense and deny doing what you know is right.
- Pride may stand in the way if you determine that you should receive better treatment from another person and stand your ground in unforgiveness.
- Maybe your willingness to serving others is clouded with pride, so you refrain from doing anything toward resolution.
- Are you drawn to people that flatter you rather than listen to sound counseling?
- Could it be that pride is so predominate in your life that you avoid being accountable for your actions?

The above references are only a few of the typical reactions and reasons (pride) why we act like we do — we are human. Pride is an enemy that uses our natural feelings and emotions to respond negatively. There is nothing unusual about that. But, when we know this is our natural response, we can guard against it and learn to and recognize and avoid its influence.

This is why God's Word can be a great deal of help. We require His help to overcome this natural enemy called pride. Humility is the opposite of pride and is a characteristic of Jesus that God wants to cultivate in our character.

Humility positions us before the Lord with a willing attitude that can catapult us away from pride into His guidance and assistance. And His Holy Spirit will empower us to accomplish just that — self-control. We can experience freedom from the consequences of pride with God's help.

My life is short compared to His, and I'm eager to learn from past humans who messed things up and what difficulties I can avoid and learn from their mistakes. Warning! We then have another opportunity to grasp God's wisdom without finding out the hard way. We can learn from our ancestors and reap the benefits! We don't have to be stupid and ignore their wrong application and failed results. We can learn from their mistakes, but it is our choice to make.

As discussed before, maybe your view of church people was one of those who believed but chose not to follow after the Lord. They wouldn't be much different from a nonbeliever because they refuse to allow the Lord to grow them up and make them more Christlike.

Sorry to say, but it happens all the time. Once we are saved, our soul and spirit belong to the Lord, so why do we still can make choices for ourselves? We aren't puppets or a robot God controls. We still have a free will to choose whatever we want.

We are created as living beings with a soul and a spirit having a free will. Our physical bodies will die when we leave this earthly existence, but our souls and spirits will go on into eternity (Philippians 3:21). We even get new bodies that can survive in eternity because our physical bodies cannot.

STAGE 4

Stage 4 means you've decided to follow after the Lord but are not willing to sell out entirely and practice His principles. You want to hold back just enough to know your saved but still want to live life your way. Not thoroughly persuaded to give up all your fleshly desires and grow from a baby Christian into a mature believing adult. It takes time to grow spiritually — just like it takes time to grow physically. Some believers are not willing to choose obedience.

Should you desire to move into Stage 5, you must decide to follow after the Lord and pursue living for the Lord as He instructs. Not doing so will keep you in Stage 4. Saved, but not living a better life that only the Lord can provide. Struggling with the consequences, that you could have avoided by choosing His help to guide you through.

There is a strong possibility many of your consequences were created by your disobedience. This is based on Scripture found in

Galatians chapter 6, verse 7. God will not be mocked and due to this fact we will reap exactly what we sow.

Many Christians today survive in this stage of life knowing their eternity is secure, but don't grow their faith by following after the Word of God. Their fire insurance policy is secured, but life remains challenging, and their example gives the world nothing different to see in their behavior and certainly nothing desirable for themselves that Christianity provides.

God's Word in action reveals His Presence working in you and provides the world around us the opportunity to see Him in action. They get to see Him working in our lives, giving others the results of what God can do with a person of faith practicing godly principles and benefiting as a direct result. It's called the Fruit of the Spirit revealed in our lives!

Faith in action is incredible because it involves the Lord providing a result that lifts us above and through difficult circumstances with provisions the world cannot experience or obtain without Him. Faith is what pleases God and opens us up to receive His help and exhibit to others the godly changes that occur in our lives.

His directed path is very different from the worlds thinking, and it produces a witness of His power and wisdom obtainable no other way. We become a visible witness of His wisdom living life to the fullest, even with all the difficult circumstances life provides.

Our choosing to follow His leading is a path of best results and progressively moves us closer to Him. This progression deepens our relationship with the Lord and changes us to exhibit a Christlike character. Our behavior reveals more of God and His nature. Allowing Him to lead gives expression to His essence, causing us to be a witness to others. Our choosing to respond in obedience allows this change in us, and is our witness to nonbelievers.

Acting out your Christian witness by trying to exhibit your own goodness rather than depend on God will certainly give others a hypocritical perspective. If this is your approach to following after the Lord lookout! Disaster is waiting in your future. When we choose this method we exhibit a form of religion the Pharisees' used and failed miserably.

Choosing to follow the Lord establishes a personal relationship with Him. His sacrifice on the cross made possible for a believing humanity to respond in obedience and receive the fulness of Christ! Trust me, His version of serving far exceeds anything we can muster us!

CHAPTER FIVE

This Gets Better all the Time!

STAGE 5

S tage 5 means you've decided to follow after the Lord and are willing to practice His principles and grow from a baby Christian into a mature believing adult. It takes time in growing spiritually — just like it takes time to grow physically. Our choosing to follow the Lord provides a whole new way to living life! Following His principles will catapult your life to new heights.

Always remember, this is a process and not an event. Growing in the Lord is similar to going to school. We progress and learn to build upon the previous grade and climb in grades and into maturity as we learn the foundational principles God desires and apply them in our lives.

It requires an open mind to the Scriptures and a renewed mind obtained from the Scriptures to get out of our natural thinking mode based on the understanding of this world — not God's. We are encouraged from Scripture to renew our minds and allow the Word of God to transform our natural thinking and learn to practice these Truths that bring wisdom, victory and success.

> Romans 12:2:
> *"Don't copy the behavior and customs of this world, but let God transform you into a new person by changing the way you think. Then you will learn to know God's will for you, which is good and pleasing and perfect."*

The bible encourages us to learn from the mistakes of others. Several examples are referenced in a variety of situations. Some biblical characters were very successful while others failed miserably. Their failures give us a glimpse of ourselves and what we can learn about our human tendencies, natural characteristics, and unscriptural principles. Understanding our nature reveals how we will react and respond naturally. This is just the ways things are!

The bible clearly shows us what to do and what not to do. This provides what our future holds based on our decisions. It isn't a book of do's and don'ts; it's a book of principles that will provide us a way of living that can improve our way of life and obtain the many blessings God offers.

Following after God's Word will provide the benefits of success and prospering that will bless our journey, and reap results that we each will enjoy. Choosing to ignore the Word of God and live in opposition will yield a curse and stagnation in our walk with Him and yield a much more difficult journey through life.

Look at the Example from Scripture found in the Old Testament

> Deuteronomy 11:26-28:
> *"Look, today I am giving you the choice between a blessing and a curse! You will be blessed if you obey the*

commands of the LORD your God that I am giving you
today. But you will be cursed if you reject the commands
of the LORD your God and turn away from him and
worship gods you have not known before."

This Scripture is often referred to as do's and don'ts, but it explains how God works. God's plans for humankind have provided a means for us to choose how we want to live our lives. It is His declaration revealing how to choose between the right and wrong approach for yourself. And what to expect depending on your choice!

These are prophetic words of wisdom telling you beforehand what will happen if you follow Him, or you don't. It's a choice we each must make for ourselves, knowing the results before our decision and what to expect.

Look in the New Testament and read for yourself these same set of plans that provide guidance and an opportunity to prosper and be in health:

Romans 6:16 reads:
"Don't you realize that you become the slaves of
whatever you choose to obey? You can be a slave to sin,
which leads to death, or you can choose to obey God,
which leads to righteous living."

Ephesians 2:2:
"You used to live in sin, just like the rest of the world,
obeying the devil — the commander of the powers in
the unseen world. He is the spirit at work in the hearts
of those who refuse to obey God."

What a descriptive word picture we see revealed from God's Word. It isn't difficult to see that our choices in life make a significant difference. Our choosing how to live our lives makes all the difference in what our future holds.

I don't want to be used of the devil while I'm here on earth. I want to be used by the Lord! If I choose not to obey Scriptures, then I'm not following the path I desire and won't get the results I don't want in my future. I want all that God offers, so I know that I must practice obedience to His Word if I want to get the rewards He offers.

I've always thought that life is still a challenge even with the Lord, but without Him — I don't want to make my circumstances more complicated than they are already. Why not select His offer and get all the help you can?

We have hit on even a broader picture in Scripture of the world we live in and how it operates. The unseen world is where we encounter evil and harassment from Satan. Having no power in the flesh to combat this force places us at its mercy and under its control. The tools to battle the evil spiritual world are found as we apply obedience to His Word.

We see that people who don't obey Scripture are subject to evil powers without any way to deal with them. This kind of living keeps us under the curse during our lifetime. And without any effective resistance to its adverse affects. Always remember that we cannot combat the unseen spiritual world we live in using our natural abilities.

Choosing to obey what Scripture teaches and trusting in the Lord Jesus Christ will deliver us from this spiritual bondage during our lifetime. And obedience to His Word and believing in Christ provides a way out and the freedom to experience the good life God intends for all humanity.

Life isn't just several designated years of living out your time here, but an opportunity to experience God's assistance all along the journey and benefit from your choices based on His Word. We really may be in training for reigning with Christ in our future.

He provides the opportunity to rise above humankind's limited natural powers and receive help from the Lord that ends in peace and joy in the Holy Spirit! This place in life is the position the Lord has made available to all believers — every last one of us!

do you want for your existence now? And, what do you want for your final destination? The choice you make now can answer both questions. Your response can change both your life now and can change where you will spend eternity.

Leaving this physical life as a believer and entering Heaven when life here on earth ends is one choice we must make. A second choice is deciding to live our lives in obedience to God's Word while we live — or not.

Stage 5 is choosing to live in obedience to God's Word and practice His principles and trust in Him by faith no matter what comes our way. A blessed life on earth is your future when choosing this path and makes for a fulfilled life as the rewards caused by obedience continue to pile up.

This choice of obedience to the Lord can be seen throughout Scripture. The following are benefits realized when obedience to the Lord is your choice:

> **Worship only God** — Leviticus 26:1:
> *"Do not make idols or set up carved images, or sacred pillars, or sculptured stones in your land so you may worship them. I am the Lord your God."*

> **Live to God** — Deuteronomy 10:12:
> *"And now, Israel, what does the Lord your God require of you? He requires only that you fear the Lord your God, and live in a way that pleases him, and love him and serve him with all your heart and soul."*

> **Obey the Word** — Deuteronomy 11:8:
> *"Therefore, be careful to obey every command I am giving you today, so you may have strength to go in and take over the land you are about to enter."* The Promised Land — our life on earth with Him as our guide.

Operate above the Natural realm — Deuteronomy 28:1:
"If you fully obey the Lord your God and carefully keep all his commands that I am giving you today, <u>the Lord your God will set you high above all the nations of the world</u>."

Obedience to God — 1 Samuel 15:22:
But Samuel replied, "What is more pleasing to the Lord: your burnt offerings and sacrifices or your obedience to his voice? Listen! Obedience is better than sacrifice, and submission is better than offering the fat of rams."

Be Rid of all that Displeased God — 2 Kings 23:24:
"Josiah also got rid of the mediums and psychics, the household gods, the idols, and every other kind of detestable practice, both in Jerusalem and throughout the land of Judah. He did this in obedience to the laws written in the scroll that Hilkiah the priest had found in the Lord's Temple."

Be Careful how you Live — 2 Chronicles 27:6:
"King Jotham became powerful because he was careful to <u>live in obedience to the Lord his God</u>."

Obey and Live the Good life — Ezekiel 20:13:
"But the people of Israel rebelled against me, and they refused to obey my decrees there in the wilderness. <u>They wouldn't obey my regulations even though obedience would have given them life.</u> They also violated my Sabbath days. So I threatened to pour out my fury on them, and I made plans to utterly consume them in the wilderness."

Fear of God is Wisdom — Haggai 1:12:
"Then Zerubbabel son of Shealtiel, and Jeshua son of Jehozadak, the high priest, and the whole remnant of

God's people began to obey the message from the Lord their God. When they heard the words of the prophet Haggai, whom the Lord their God had sent, <u>the people feared the Lord.</u>"

A Relationship by Faith brings Obedience — Romans 4:13:
"Clearly, God's promise to give the whole earth to Abraham and his descendants was based not on his obedience to God's law, but <u>on a right relationship with God that comes by faith</u>."

Christ made us Right through His Obedience — Romans 10:5:
"For Moses writes that the law's way of making a person right with God <u>requires obedience to all of its commands</u>."

Today we live in the existence of God's grace which is acceptance by faith rather than living by a set of laws or rules to follow.

Learn Obedience by Example — Hebrews 5:8:
"Even though Jesus was God's Son, <u>he learned obedience</u> from the things he suffered."

See How the Lord Values our Acceptance of Him

John 14:21:
"Those who accept my commandments and obey them are the ones who love me. And because they love me, my Father will love them. And I will love them and reveal myself to each of them."

Obedience to the Word of God causes our faith to grow. It spiritually draws us closer to Him, and it builds trust in what He says. Obedience positions us closer to the Lord and deepens our relationship with Him.

Our choice to follow His principles and teaching brings His Presence into our lives and makes Him more real in the process!

Does this sound rigid or legalistic and cause you to call it rules and strict regulations? If it were, then legalism would enter the definition rather than a love relationship with the Lord. Love is a byproduct of knowing the Lord, personally, and developing a relationship with Him!

A relationship with the Lord is our responding in obedience because we want to please Him — not because we need to mind a set of rules so He will be happy with our actions. A love relationship does not include following regimented rules. A love relationship is willfully serving a God that has infiltrated our spirit and lives and wants to be in a relationship with us.

The Ten Commandments set a standard that revealed what was required by God to be acceptable to Him, but humanity could not live and obey each one. This is not humanly possible. Knowing this fact, what did God do?

God Provided the Law to reveal Sin to Humanity

> Romans 3:20:
> *"For no one can ever be made right with God by doing what the law commands. The law simply shows us how sinful we are."*

> Romans 5:20:
> *"God's law was given so that all people could see how sinful they were. But as people sinned more and more, God's wonderful grace became more abundant."*

As a Result of Failing to Meet the Requirements of the Law

> Galatians 2:16:
> *"Yet we know that a person is made right with God by faith in Jesus Christ, not by obeying the law. And we have believed in Christ Jesus, so that we might be*

made right with God because of our faith in Christ, not because we have obeyed the law. For no one will ever be made right with God by obeying the law."

The religious establishment tried to live according to each of the Ten Commandment, but was not successful. Those who still try today live a legalistic lifestyle that sets in judgment of others who are less successful at living-out the law. This religious approach leaves no room for error and introduces a human-made religion which no one can be successful at doing (Romans 4:15).

So What Was God's Solution?

2 Corinthians 3:6:
"He has enabled us to be ministers of his new covenant. This is a covenant not of written laws, but of the Spirit. The old written covenant ends in death; but under the new covenant, the Spirit gives life."

Grace was Introduced to Make a Way for Us

John 1:17:
"For the law was given through Moses, but God's unfailing love and faithfulness came through Jesus Christ."

Acts 13:39:
"Everyone who believes in him is made right in God's sight—something the law of Moses could never do."

Galatians 2:21:
"I do not treat the grace of God as meaningless. For if keeping the law could make us right with God, then there was no need for Christ to die."

Did we Have to Do Anything to Earn God's Acceptance?

Romans 3:27:
"Can we boast, then, that we have done anything to be accepted by God? No, because our acquittal is not based on obeying the law. It is based on faith."

Does Faith then Block Out the Law?

Romans 3:31:
"Well then, if we emphasize faith, does this mean that we can forget about the law? Of course not! In fact, <u>only when we have faith do we truly fulfill the law.</u>"

How Does Grace Fit Into This Solution?

Romans 6:14:
"Sin is no longer your master, for you no longer live under the requirements of the law. Instead, you live under the freedom of God's grace."

Does Accepting Jesus by Faith Remove the Curse?

Galatians 3:10:
"But those who depend on the law to make them right with God are under his curse, for the Scriptures say, 'Cursed is everyone who does not observe and obey all the commands that are written in God's Book of the Law.'"

Galatians 3:11:
"So it is clear that no one can be made right with God by trying to keep the law. For the Scriptures say, <u>It is through faith that a righteous person has life.</u>"

Then God sent His Son to meet every condition needed to satisfy God's penalty for sin. Jesus fulfilled all the requirements and satisfied the sentence imposed by God when He sacrificed Himself to God and paid our sin debt when we were all born.

> Matthew 5:17:
> *"Don't misunderstand why I have come. I did not come to abolish the law of Moses or the writings of the prophets. No, I came to accomplish their purpose."*

> Acts 13:39:
> *"Everyone who believes in him is made right in God's sight—something the law of Moses could never do."*

> Romans 3:28:
> *"So we are made right with God through faith and not by obeying the law."*

Jesus satisfied God's penalty for sin once and for all. That was completed on the Cross by Christ. His act of obedience opened the door to the Father, so we can have fellowship with Him rather than follow a regiment of rules. Thus, faith became our avenue to receive grace and be pardoned for the sin that once overshadowed our unrighteous status.

Knowing humanity was unable to fulfill the Ten Commandment, He realized that something more was needed to resolve the sin penalty. Therefore, Christ was ready and willing to sacrifice Himself in our place to bring humanity back into good standing with the Father. As you can see, from God's awareness He created our option to escape sin's penalty by faith!

Accepting Christ and what He has done to remove this penalty puts us in good standing with the Father like it was before sin entered the world in the Garden. It resolves the sin issue once blocking our access to God the Father. By faith, we now become the righteousness of God in Christ, and our position with God is entirely new and open for fellowship.

If we choose not to accept Christ and what He has done, then the sin issue remains, and we are not able to fellowship with God. We are at enmity still and will remain in the unacceptable state until we accept Christ and receive what He has done for all humanity. Without accepting Christ by faith, we remain under the law and will be condemned by it.

Christ is our opportunity to breach the sin gap and come into a right relationship with our Creator. It is the only way to God the Father (John 14:6). Our attempts without the Cross are futile, and we can be as religious as we want, but that changes nothing concerning the sin issue.

Our obedience to Scripture must begin with our Salvation and acceptance of Jesus as our Savior and Lord. That one act by faith, that single choice, begins our walk with the Lord and opens up a new life for us unseen until that decision.

Take a look at what Jesus did as He carried out His purpose for coming to earth. His journey required obedience, so all that was prophesied in the Old Testament took place. This action by Christ gave results to God's Word previously spoken to man and became a reality. Jesus had to follow through so that Scripture would be fulfilled. So, what did Jesus do?

> Luke 9:51:
> *"Now it came to pass, when the time had come for Him to be received up, that He steadfastly set His face to go to Jerusalem."*

What is being said here is a great lesson and example for us to follow? This Scripture is relating to Jesus and the subsequent event of His crucifixion. His time to head for Jerusalem to be sacrificed on the Cross for our sins was at hand.

What did Jesus do? He set His face to go to Jerusalem. Setting His face involved making the decision to move in location and determine that He would follow His Father's will and sacrifice Himself to fulfill the Father's will and provide Salvation for all humankind. Jesus had to pay attention that nothing got in the way of Him fulfilling the purpose for His coming into the world.

With all that was ahead of Him — Calvary, it would have been easy to put things off and delay this horrible death and crucifixion that awaited Him. Our example of Jesus and His determination to please the Father and complete the goal set before Him was intentional with great purpose and faithfulness of character in order to accomplish His mission.

Our purpose in life is to be obedient to Scripture as we develop our love relationship with the Lord. Our persistence and willingness to be changed in character to become Christlike is essential to follow His path.

This thinking is where God is calling all of us. We need to be determined that we will not be sidetracked and lose sight of God's goal. Our delay will change the right timing for success, and if we loose focus or become disobedient, we could miss out altogether.

When God has provided us an opportunity to journey through life with Him, we should respond with unwavering obedience to His every word. God's will for you is contained in the bible, and your designated path to follow is woven throughout all of Scripture. Stop asking God's will for you and set your face on Him no matter what (Proverbs 4:25).

Obedience to God's Word is necessary to follow His leading and to receive the Holy Spirit's power. We each need to be victorious during our lifetime to achieve His fullness. Anything other than obedience is called disobedience, which takes you entirely out of His care and guidance.

Look what Christ did as He Followed after God's Leading

> Hebrews 5:8:
> *"Even though Jesus was God's Son, he learned obedience from the things he suffered."*

Our greatest challenge in life will be to follow in obedience after God's Word, no matter what. God never excuses disobedience anywhere in Scripture. A sure way to stay on track is to do all that you know to do that is right, and then, because of your obedience, God's next instruction will soon follow.

In reading a section from Day by Day, page 42, written by Dr. Henry Blackaby and his son Richard, the cause of following the Lord out of love rather than discipline alone is given. It reads as follows:

Love Brings Obedience

> *"Obedience to God's commands comes from your heart. When you begin struggling to obey God, that is a clear indication your heart has shifted away from Him. Some claim: "I love God, but I'm having difficulty obeying Him in certain areas of my life." That is a spiritual impossibility. If I were to ask you, "Do you love God?" you might respond "Yes!" However, if I were to ask you, "Are you obeying God?" would you answer yes as quickly?"*
>
> *Yet I would be asking you the same question! <u>Genuine love for God leads to wholehearted obedience</u>. If you told your spouse that you loved her at certain times but that you struggled to love her at others, your relationship would be in jeopardy. Yet we assume that God is satisfied with occasional love or partial obedience. He is not.*
>
> *<u>Obedience without love is legalism</u>. Obedience for its own sake can be nothing more than perfectionism, which leads to pride. Many conscientious Christians seek to cultivate discipline in their lives to be more obedient to Christ. As helpful as spiritual disciplines can be, they never can replace your love for God. <u>Love is the discipline</u>. God looks beyond your church*

involvement and focuses His penetrating gaze upon your heart.

Has your worship become empty and routine? Have you lost your motivation to read God's Word? 'are you experiencing spiritual lethargy? Is your prayer life reduced to a ritual? These are symptoms of a heart that has shifted away from God. Return to your first love. <u>Love is the greatest motivation for a relationship with God and for serving Him</u>.'"

Love must be our motivation, or else legalism will prevail. God is love (agape), and His kind of love (unconditional) deviates from the love we know in the natural realm. His love brings with it the power of the Holy Spirit and transcends all that we can try to muster up. His love will bring motivation and an eagerness to our Spirit that will overshadow our selfish desires if we will but turn Him loose.

Our inner being, our Spirit, will be urged to follow after the One true God that desires a relationship with His creation. We, the highlight of His design, can have a relationship with our Creator personally. The Lord reaches down to all humankind and offers us Himself to receive a love otherwise unknown to man.

Consider your options and choose the God of all gods — the Creator of all who wants to be in relationship with you. Do it while you can and before your journey through life ends. It — the end — will be here before you know it. Determine to serve Him above all else and enjoy your life on earth while you still can.

Pursue His Presence and experience Him during your journey through Stage 5 and enjoy the good life God intended for you. That choice will fulfill His plan for you and keep you directly in His Will.

CHAPTER SIX

I Didn't Know this was Even Possible!

So, what is Stage 6 then? Is there more to living on earth than I first thought? Yes, there is. Learning and growing and depending on the Lord will change you into a sacrificial offering to the Lord, just like a sacrifice in the Old Testament. Choosing to place yourself on the altar before the Lord is choosing to serve Him — without limitations (Romans 12:1).

— STAGE 6

Stage 6 means you've decided to follow after the Lord and are willing to practice His principles and grow from a baby Christian into a mature believing adult. It takes time in growing spiritually — just like it takes time to grow physically. Not a cabana boy either, so drop that concept. It is cooperating with the guidance of the Holy Spirit's guidance while putting into practice the principles in your lifestyle and allowing Him to work them out in your life — no matter what!

Learning to apply His wisdom is not a natural occurrence, nor does it take place by itself. Our instincts are contrary to following anyone except ourselves. So, we must purpose to seek the Lord in our life and remain determined to find out how far He will take us.

There is no end to His wisdom, so even at life's end, there will be much more we could have learned. It depends on how we hang in there and pursue Him until our life is physically over. I'm wanting to live a long time so I can see how far I can go with Him and get to know Him better and better during my lifetime.

This relationship has taken me to places I knew nothing about, and with new lessons to learn and people to meet, and tasks to tackle are endless. The more I learn about Him, the more I realize I have minimal knowledge about much of anything.

It seems like the more I know, the more I have yet to gather. Why? Because the volume of things to come from Him are limitless. The horizon continues to expand, and He is offering so much that it overwhelms my natural thinking. This knowledge causes excitement within me and an even greater desire to learn more. I need to give it all I can because there is so much I don't know regarding His wisdom!

Experiencing God is a journey not obtainable following man's ways. One can't just take off to expand their spiritual wisdom and divine knowledge without His assistance. This dependency on Him provides the avenue to obtain the power to learn godly wisdom. The bible calls its value *greater than silver or gold!* Not something we can accomplish on our own. His Holy Spirit, the Spirit of God living in us, is endless in His ability and guidance. I need to get to know Him better and learn His ways in greater detail.

It all starts when we decide to make Jesus the Lord of our life as a believer. This lordship is a choice on our part to accept Him and allow Him to guide, commune, instruct, and change us into the likeness of Christ His Son. This choosing is a conscious effort on our part as we extend our *free will* to obtain all God has for us in this life.

Doing so involves us putting into practice His principles as provided in the bible and practice them in our daily living. Looking at Scripture to elaborate this point see the following references:

Galatians 4:3 & 9:

"And that's the way it was with us before Christ came. We were like children; we were slaves to the basic spiritual principles of this world."

"So now that you know God (or should I say, now that God knows you), why do you want to go back again and become slaves once more to the weak and useless spiritual principles of this world?"

Check out Scripture that supports this path and grasp the will of God in your own life. This offer is extended to all humanity without any exceptions (Acts 10:34). There is no favoritisms with God. *He does not discriminate!*

We argue so much about the color of our skin, the location where we live, the car we drive, the neighborhood where we reside, our job title, and so many things that mean nothing to our God. Humanities' self-evaluation is pitiful as we compare one with the other. God does not evaluate humanity regarding any of these difference!

The Lord gave me a vision once, using a chessboard to observe individuals standing upright. When viewed from the side, each person was different in height, size, title, etc. The height of the people was based on their individual merits, education, wealth, etc., as we see each other from our worldly perspective.

Then, the Lord gave me a view from His perspective — looking from above — down on the chessboard. In looking down from overhead, I could not tell one person from another. Each person looked just alike and there were no differences! Could it be we need a new perspective of how we evaluate one another?

He wants everyone to obtain the fullness of His grace and mercy. He wants us to work with Him no matter what part of society we live. His concern isn't for a specific accomplishment that makes you better, or higher, or more important than someone else. It is to become the best at what God created you be, and to be yourself following after Him!

You don't have to provide a list of degrees, various levels of education, a specific field of endeavor, or get your life all together, so you're acceptable to Him. He want's you right where you are, and absolutely nothing will stand in your way as you reach out to Him. He knows you better than you know yourself. God doesn't need someone to tell Him how valuable you are — He already knows!

Remember, He knit you together in your mother's womb. He knows your human, and that's not a problem. He is aware you have a sinful nature, and without Him, you can't accomplish what He wants you to do. This deficiency does not make Him love you any less or more than He already does. God's agape love is unconditional!

His kind of love (agape) is not easily understood. How could anybody love anyone as He does? No one can. We must believe in Him by faith and not relate Him to our earthly fathers, or we'll sell ourselves short. The love of God the Father is so enormous it far exceeds anything we can conceive or fully understand.

So — What is this Agape Love anyway?

The Wikipedia definition is quoted as follows:

Agape (Ancient Greek ἀγάπη, agapē) is a Greco-Christian term referring to love, "The highest form of love, charity" and "the love of God for man". The word is not to be confused with philia, brotherly love, or philautia, self-love, as it embraces a universal, unconditional love that transcends and persists regardless of circumstance. It goes beyond just the emotions to the extent of seeking the best for others.

Some authors make a distinction between the two following thoughts:

Unconditional love is "given freely" to the loved one "no matter what". Loving is primary. It is seen as infinite and measureless.

Conditional love is 'earned' on the basis of conscious or unconscious conditions being met by the lover. Conditional love requires some kind of finite exchange.

Reference to the love of God is found throughout Scripture. Scripture even tells us that God is Love (1 John 4:8). So, is this kind of love different from what we experience as human beings? It must be important because love is mentioned 759 times in the New Living Translation of the bible!

Check out the Following Scriptures and See how God's Love is Used

Deuteronomy 6:5:
"And you must love the Lord your God with all your heart, all your soul, and all your strength."

Deuteronomy 7:9:
"Understand, therefore, that the Lord your God is indeed God. He is the faithful God who keeps his covenant for a thousand generations and lavishes his unfailing love on those who love him and obey his commands."

Matthew 5:43-44:
"You have heard the law that says, 'Love your neighbor' and hate your enemy. But I say, love your enemies! Pray for those who persecute you!"

John 1:17:
"For the law was given through Moses, but God's unfailing love and faithfulness came through Jesus Christ."\

Now, I want to Show you a Deeper look into God's Love

John 21:15-17:
"After breakfast Jesus asked Simon Peter, 'Simon son of John, do you (agape) love me more than these?' "Yes, Lord," Peter replied, "you know I love you." "Then feed my lambs," Jesus told him."

> *"Jesus repeated the question: 'Simon son of John, do you (agape) love me?' "Yes, Lord," Peter said, "you know I love you." "Then take care of my sheep," Jesus said.*
>
> *"A third time he asked him, 'Simon son of John, do you (phileo) love me?' Peter was hurt that Jesus asked the question a third time. He said, "Lord, you know everything. You know that I love you. Jesus said, "Then feed my sheep."*

Did the Lord really ask Peter the same question three times? It certainly appears so if you focus on the wording and Peter's concerned reply. But, is there more to that question that's hidden but intended? Yes, there is more to this question.

Take a look at the Greek word for love. The Greek language has different meanings for the word love as spoken here. As you investigate the several meanings, you find there are two different Greek words used to express love used in these verses. The translation into English provides love with only one meaning. But, the original Greek is more precise in meaning and gives us a broader understanding to its particular application that is lost in the translation.

The two Greek words used in this Scripture can be seen very different as the definition for each is provided. In verses 15 and 16, the same Greek word *agape* (love) is used. In verse 17, the Greek word *phileo (love)* is used. By definition, each Greek word is used for a reason and provides a much broader meaning to these verses as used here.

Agape love indicates more than human feelings of friendship, and it is not a physical attraction for another person. Agape love is not the liking of a person, which is how the word phileo (love) is intended. Agape love is a much different kind of love, and only through God can this kind of love be obtained or experienced.

I use the word obtained because only through the power of the Holy Spirit working inside of each believer can we experience agape love. Agape love is a divine kind of unconditional love that does not vary based on circumstances, feelings, emotions, or fondness of one person with another. It is consistent, a deep unconditional love — No matter what! Absolutely nothing can change this kind of love. It isn't earned either. God's agape love is extended to all of humanity equally with no restrictions or conditions!

It is the purist form of love and is a direct representation of God's character as He exists and functions. Everything God does evolves from this kind of perfect love and is the very best and forgiving for all involved. God is always focusing on the condition of our heart, and His form of love is the highest form known. His motives are pure and for our best interest — always!

His agape love does not eliminate phileo love — it only reveals a kind of love that cannot be experienced without Him as the source. It is not an elevated form of phileo love, but rather a sincere, caring, powerful love that is totally unconditional and found only in Him and through His Holy Spirit that makes it real in our lives.

In verses 15 and 16, we see the Lord is asking Simon Peter if he has the love (agape) only God can give. Peter is not understanding because he believes that Jesus is asking him the same question three times. In fact, Peter has interpreted love in the only way he knows it — (phileo) love. So what's the problem?

The problem is that Peter has not yet received the Holy Spirit and does not understand or is capable of agape love. It is not humanly possible to receive or understand what only God can provide through the power of the Holy Spirit.

We must have the Holy Spirit living on the inside of us to grasp a love greater than our human emotions and feelings can imagine. Agape love is not based on feelings and emotions but on unconditional love that is never wavering, fault-finding, biased or conditional. It is pure love (agape) that transcends phileo love as found in humanity.

How do I know this? I know this because I see in referencing back to the original language that love has more than one meaning. The original language is more descriptive than our English language. I see these three verses in John, chapter 21:15-17, having three questions having two different meanings of the word love. As a result, agape love has additional meaning that Peter not is not understanding. I see the Lord is showing Peter; it takes more than the human ability to understand what the Lord is saying.

We aren't any different today. We each need the presence and power of the Holy Spirit in our lives to better understand what God is telling us and what He wants us to be doing. This is one of His communication methods, and we must position ourselves in Christ to breach the gap caused by sin to reach our Creator in real-time.

Take a look at the Book of Acts in the New Testament. You will find throughout Acts mention of the Holy Spirit. After Christ left the earth, His coming revealed a marked difference in the believers who received Him (Acts 4:31).

When the Holy Spirit comes into the scene, sent by Christ after He left earth, power from God will be experienced (Acts 1:8). That's exactly what happened to the 120 who waited in the upper room (Acts 2:1). They waited and received from God the Holy Spirit promised when Jesus returned to the Father (Acts 2:4). This is the Comforter (Advocate or Holy Spirit) Jesus promised He would send once He departed and went back to sit at the right hand of God (John 15:26; 16:5-7).

In Acts 4:8, Peter began the ministry God intended for him as he spoke under the influence God promised to provide. That influence was the Holy Spirit! As you can see in other Scriptures, Peter was eager to please Jesus during their walk together on earth, as witnessed by his many human thoughts, actions, comments, and blurting out his feelings and emotions without any promptings from the Lord. This was the real Peter, as his natural self, without the Holy Spirit working in his life just like we are without guidance and power from the Lord.

But, once Peter received the power from on high, the Holy Spirit, his whole life changed. His spirit began to operate to God's promptings, and as a result, Peter was motivated by the Lord rather than reacting to his own feelings and emotions alone. Nothing is any different today for each of us.

Those disciples of old were just ordinary human beings with life issues of their own and the normalcy of expressing their opinions and thinking. They were walking with Jesus, and they were learning His ways, but they were not yet motivated by the promptings of the Lord as the Holy Spirit directed.

Please read the following, *"Resumes of Apostles"* taken off the internet and see how the application for a position to be a disciple with Jesus might take place in today's world:

Resumes of Apostles

To: Jesus, Son of Joseph
Woodcrafter's Carpenter Shop
Nazareth 25922

From: Jordan Management Consultants

Dear Sir:

Thank you for submitting the resumes of the twelve men you have picked for managerial positions in your new organization. All of them have now taken our battery of tests; and we have not only run the results through our computer, but also arranged personal interviews for each of them with our psychologist and vocational aptitude consultant.

The profiles of all tests are included, and you will want to study each of them carefully. As part of our service, we make some general comments for your guidance, much as an auditor will include some general statements. This is given as a result of staff consultation, and comes without any additional fee.

It is the staff opinion that most of your nominees are lacking in background, education and vocational aptitude for the type of enterprise you are undertaking. They do not have the team concept. We would recommend that you continue your search for persons of experience in managerial ability and proven capability.

Simon Peter is emotionally unstable and given to fits of temper. Andrew has absolutely no qualities of leadership. The two brothers, James and John, the sons of Zebedee, place personal interest above company loyalty.

Thomas demonstrates a questioning attitude that would tend to undermine morale. We feel that it is our duty to tell you that Matthew had been blacklisted by the Greater Jerusalem Better Business Bureau; James, the son of Alphaeus, and Thaddaeus definitely have radical leanings, and they both registered a high score on the manic-depressive scale.

One of the candidates, however, shows great potential. He is a man of ability and resourcefulness, meets people well, has a keen business mind, and has contacts in high places.

He is highly motivated, ambitious, and responsible. We recommend Judas Iscariot as your controller and right-hand man. All of the other profiles are self-explanatory.

We wish you every success in your new venture.

Sincerely,
Jordan Management Consultants

Eating Problems for Breakfast by Tim Hansel, Word Publishing, 1988, pp. 194-195

To assume the disciples were somehow super-human, will cause you to falter in thinking they were any different from each of us today. Knowing they were human, just like we are, can help to see their reactions with Jesus. They got to walk with Jesus in the flesh is what's different. They realized who He was and somewhat why He had come to earth, but until they received the Holy Spirit, they were without the power of God working in their lives.

God had revealed that Jesus was the Christ to come, but they had not yet experienced the presence of the Holy Spirit working from within. Their advantage over us was they got to walk and talk with Jesus in the natural. Our advantage is having the messenger of God reveal His heart, and that empowers, guides, and gives us wisdom beyond ourselves! His Spirit living inside of us is a connection the disciples never experienced until Jesus sent the Holy Spirit after His Resurrection.

To experience God's presence requires us to get in touch with the Holy Spirit that is alive inside each believer. His power source is very capable to guide, prompt, reveal, and convict us as we learn to depend on Him for help. Scripture refers to the Holy Spirit as God's appointed teacher and comforter (1 John 2:27). This source of God's help develops His kind of love (agape) in us as we follow Him.

The more we follow the Holy Spirit's guidance, the more we will experience the power of God working in us. The more we will witness the gifts God wants to see in our behavior and our actions toward humanity. The many talents of God are there to be used and exposed as we learn to function under the Holy Spirit's guidance and power.

When you accepted Christ into your life, God's Holy Spirit entered. This explains how the Lord lives inside of each believer. When I was a child, I couldn't figure out how in the world Christ could live inside of me and everyone else at the same time? Learning that my acceptance of the Lord was when the Holy Spirit entered my life was a welcomed knowledge.

But, Christ is still in heaven seated at the right hand of the Father. It just didn't make sense to me until I learned about the Holy Spirit.

Then, I started to understand there was more to this Father, Son, and Holy Spirit than I first thought. Living on the inside of a believer was possible because God's Spirit was placed there to empower us to do His Will if we choose to follow His principles and direction. Now — mystery solved!

Three in One was hard to grasp as well. As I grew in the Lord and learned to fellowship with Him, the light started shinning inside of me. I became comfortable with a living God who exists in three different forms but is one personality utilized in three separate entities and function as One. See in Appendix II, a diagram showing my attempt to better understand from Scripture about God and the concept of the Trinity.

As I grew from infancy into childhood then on into an adult believer, Scripture became easier to apply and understand. I needed terribly to be educated, and the Holy Spirit, who expresses and knows the heart of God, was given a warm welcome to guide me through my existence and allow me to experience an abundant life never before thought possible.

This following after Scripture and putting God's principles into application moved me into Stage 5, which is a marvelous change from what the world offers. Realizing there was more than just being saved — is as good as it can get on earth. God has made available everything I need to survive, conquer, and soar above life like an eagle.

Reading about the characteristic of an eagle is very interesting. Why was an eagle referred to in Scripture? When storms come, the eagle flies above the harsh environment (storm) it encounters. The fierce winds, pounding rain, lighting, thunder, and hail are still taking place, so it flies higher to avoid as much of the storm as possible. Where we choose to focus our attention and who we depend upon directly affects our spiritual altitude concerning the storms of life.

Circumstances will still be taking place, but our faith and trust in the Lord can help us rise above them and provides an easier way to get though life, knowing our God sees and knows all that is going on and will travel through with us. We always have Him with us, and He knows what lies ahead and will help us manage during any circumstances that come our way!

Knowing this about Him and the many provisions He makes available in Scripture provides a means to better understand what needs to be done to get through. I'm not advocating we dismiss or try to ignore problems or difficult circumstances, but having a Helper and applying biblical principles will give us wisdom beyond our thinking and abilities that are very comforting.

There are times in life that may bring tragedy, heartbreak, and grief-stricken moments. Still, they can be accompanied by His provisions, care, and wisdom that surpass anything I've ever considered before or experienced.

When my wife died after a 47-year courtship and marriage, it set me back emotionally and spiritually. I was suddenly without her, and having the Lord close by gave me courage and the strength I needed to know all was in His control, and I needed to trust Him.

I still experienced many adverse and uncomfortable circumstances, but I was able to see my situation through a spiritual set of eyes that encouraged me during it all. As I depended on Him during this difficult time, my spirit was rejuvenated by His Presence and continued comfort. His Presence brought comfort and peace to my grieving spirit.

During this time of loss and grief, I was heavily drugged with pain-killers because I was dealing with a very painful infection in my spine. This made the journey beyond my ability to cope. In addition to all of this, my son had seven heart attacks and was not expected to survive. This all occurred during a four month period of my life. I discovered this was not something I wanted to experience or deal with. I did not knowingly sign up for this! It was another suddenly that life can throw your way!

In fact, I had planned a trip by motorcycle through the Smoky Mountains for several hundred miles, back through West Virginia for a summer festival, then returning home full of new experiences, and new friends I'd met along the way. We had planned to camp out most of the journey and enjoy the out of doors. We wanted to enjoy the surroundings and stimulate our thoughts and senses through this beautiful area of our country.

Instead, this time frame brought sickness, death, and overwhelming circumstances never thought possible or would ever be in my lifetime. Isn't it amazing how things can change so quickly? I'm glad I don't know the future because I might choose to skip a few parts and bypass the misery.

Knowing the Lord was present was just what I needed to move forward. It was not the time to slip back into my understanding. It was not the time to rely on feelings and emotions or focus on what happened and why? It was a time to lean heavily on the Lord, and I was well aware that I could not journey alone during this painful and confusing period. I knew for sure I needed Him, and He was faithful to power me through it all.

There were days I could not walk but a short distance, and I was angry I couldn't do better. Depending on the Lord didn't make me walk any better or any farther, but it gave me a great deal of hope and peace in what He had in store for me in the future. At one point, I wasn't sure if I would make it, but since I was still alive — something was in my future and death, wasn't it.

My expectations grew because I knew my future was in His hands, and He would provide the means to flourish and grow in faith as a believer because this would pass, and life would go on with this season for growing to make me stronger.

Each stage of life is filled with seasons and unforeseen events. Your age will definitely affect many of the seasons that you will experience in life. For example, when you are young (0-18) years of age, many events will occur. Different levels of schooling will take place, accompanied by challenges and struggles. A job can happen, the responsibility of driving a car, dating, preparation for a particular career, and even a choice to serve our country in the United States Military.

You will certainly experience different phases, all during each season of development — that is for sure. This is good because it allows us to learn and grow in our knowledge and understanding of new and exciting things life brings our way. A season of experience can strengthen us to surge forward, developing wisdom as we go.

Middle age will provide many seasons — (19-65) years of age — that are common to each person depending on their profession, work ethics, type of people you are around, and lifestyle that suits you best and your specific age. Growing older changes your physical abilities and provides more opportunities to meet new challenges.

Don't wait until you're old to experience life because age lengthens the time for healing. I had 3 identical operations during my lifetime to solve a reoccurring problem. Each procedure was identical, but I received each at a different age, and that made all the difference in the time it took to heal.

I learned that I could not physically repeat at 50 what was easy for me at 25. My mind didn't age with my body, so I had to determine I was physically changing and stop those activities that would harm my body. In addition, I found that I became restricted because my stamina changed too, and I had to start taking breaks in my activities to maintain enough strength to follow through.

I recently agreed to stop going on the roof to clean out gutters, wash the skylight, blowing leaves off the roof, or trim a tree that was close to the house. This new approach wasn't wrong, but not to my liking. But, I complied and hired some help to accomplish this result to satisfy my wife.

My only retaliation was a facial frown with my full compliance to follow. I did find a fun way to help me get back on the roof when a tree recently fell. I purchased a drone that would allow me to enjoy my continuing childhood and survey the roof for damage all at the same time.

Why not? Should I need pictures to send the insurance company I can provide them with a birds-eye view and remain in full compliance with my wife's wishes. So, problem solved and a new toy to entertain me combined with my mature approach and problem-solving skills.

When the older years move in, your seasons will still come, but they will change again, just like the other life stages. They will be customized to your physical and mental health, available income, lifestyle, personal growth, and maturity. Maybe there's a drone in your future?

Each season of each age group and stage we move through will provide numerous opportunities and require choices that will build, one upon the other, and guide the direction we each choose to travel. Should you want your life without the Lord, then different events will take place, and they will materialize and formulate your future.

Should you choose the Lord to be in your life, then added opportunities can be accessed that are not available to the secular individual that remains on his own. Remember, you choose which path to take in life, and you are singly responsible for your selection.

Choosing the Lord has its many facets and levels of living, just like choosing to follow your path and dealing with circumstances by yourself. Similar events will happen that are common during your existence, but your approach to dealing with them can include help from a different group of solutions when the Lord is involved.

We each are given this freedom to choose a path, and each will have its consequences. On the one hand, choosing the path of your own doing will present itself with problems that you will struggle without the Lord's help. In like manner, if you choose to follow the Lord, then the spiritual realm of your existence will have options to combat against circumstances where the natural approach (your chosen path) will not receive any help from the Lord. You are on your own.

Now, since humanity cannot battle against the forces in the spiritual realm, we are left to war against a force we cannot see and have no power to combat. We are powerless against spiritual forces surrounding our existence. This is crippling to humankind and leaves us void of any defense and the ability to protect ourselves from satanic attacks. It leaves us in a position of fallen man that we were born into when we entered the world at birth. There are no physical weapons available that can combat the spiritual world!

God knew that fallen man was put in this position all because of the sin committed by Adam and Eve in the Garden of Eden. This known fact is the reason why God provided His Son to redeem humanity from this condition. Christ came to give us a choice that was not available while we were living in the sinful condition in which we were born.

When we choose to accept Jesus into our lives as our savior, we have chosen the path to be released from sin's destination. That's all that must be done to obtain a righteous status with God. It is a simple fact that we individually must choose to receive the benefits of Salvation (Hebrews 9:26 & 10:5).

Stage 4 positions us to communicate with the Holy Spirit, and is how we are considered to have the Spirit of God dwelling in us. As I said before, when you first heard that Christ lives in you and didn't understand — well, now you do. The Spirit of God comes alive within us!

The Holy Spirit also provides the power of God necessary to assist us spiritually in the physical realm we now live. When this access to God's power is released, it provides everything we need to learn and practice the principles of God. We soon learn we are given the ability to read the bible with greater understanding. Remember, before the Lord, how difficult the bible was to read and understand?

This new internal power from the Lord, the Holy Spirit, will open up your understanding of the instructions from reading God's Word. This new set of spiritual eyes provides what each of us need to take in and allow Him to renew our minds and change our thinking (our vs. His thinking) and get us on the same page as Him!

So, being in Stage 4 can be a place where we can remain saved. But, if we don't utilize what the Lord has made available to help us, then we will remain saved but facing life without growing and maturing in the Lord. This is a miserable place to remain, but many people choose this path. Don't be one of them.

They proceed through life without any help from God because they have determined to do it by themselves. They may not even be aware that the Lord is readily available. When the Israelites were traveling to the Promised Land, they too chose to do life on their own. This left them in the desert, a very harsh environment that caused them to have many problems that could have been avoided had they chosen God's directing and power instead.

It's good to be saved from the consequences of sin, but it still allows difficulties and harsh circumstances to continually surround you while traveling on life's journey. A miserable journey that can be significantly enhanced by choosing God as our tour guide. This directing from our tour guide, the Lord, will add help and assistance all during the journey resulting in a life being easier to maneuver and enjoy more fully!

Our guidebook, the bible, provides tremendous wisdom for our journey. Choosing not to follow its many applications and principles cheats us out of the blessed lifestyle God intends.

While growing up, maybe your family had a bible lying on the coffee table in the living room. This was common when I grew up and always caused me to wonder if it ever got opened. Why? Because the folks usually had select photos placed strategically in the pages or a smashed flower from so and so's wedding or funeral. Maybe your family bible had a graduation picture received from a special relative as a gift. Do I hear any bells going off?

When I started reading it, I discovered it was heavy and awkward to handle and best left lying right where it was. The King James version was hard for me to understand, and with all the graphic pictures, a variety of fancy fonts — well, it seemed to be for pretty and not for use. The pictures were great, though, but the smashed flowers were too much.

When all the different bible translations became available, I was amazed to read and better understand what was being said. My progress continued, and over the years, I have obtained surprising wisdom from reading the Word of God! Plus, no flowers have been needed to stain the pages — just the Holy Spirit!

Yes, we believers still have demanding circumstances and

barriers to overcome in life. With the Lord's help, our progression is continual, and our applications of Scripture to each event will provide tremendous aid to lighten our difficulties. Besides, any difficulties in the spiritual realm can be met with God's armor, as explained in chapter 6 of Ephesians.

Our difficulties with emotions and feelings can be lessened as we learn to apply His principles. Should we take the path alone our journey will be very different. His assistance will lighten our burdens, provide hope all during our travels, and give us a more excellent life that is more enjoyable and rewarding.

Should you choose to incorporate His guidance and apply His principles to your everyday life, you will enter Stage 5, which is satisfying and very rewarding. This stage is where the Lord wants us to move into and reap the many gifts and bonuses not available in any other stage.

Life in Stage 5 allows us to receive theses many gifts that God provides though the power of His Holy Spirit. Divine power not obtainable any other way. The numerous promises of God can be experienced as we spend time in Stage 5, and remain focused on the Lord.

God has chosen to save His believing children and shower them with gifts from above. He challenges us to turn Him loose with our finances so He can bless us. This is the only place in the bible where God challenges us to test Him. Take a look at the Scripture that follows:

> Malachi 3:8-10:
> *"Should people cheat God? Yet you have cheated me! But you ask, 'What do you mean? When did we ever cheat you?' "You have cheated me of the tithes and offerings due to me."*
>
> *"You are under a curse, for your whole nation has been cheating me."*
>
> *"Bring all the tithes into the storehouse so there will be enough food in my Temple. If you do," says the*

Lord of Heaven's Armies, "I will open the windows of heaven for you. I will pour out a blessing so great you won't have enough room to take it in! Try it! Put me to the test!"

This 'test' is not that difficult because it is based on faith and trust in Him and His Word. When we do what He says, then He does the rest. When God says, test me, this is an activity where you can't lose. His unseen presence will cause you to witness His activity in your finances you did not think existed or possible. And very likely, it will bring amazement to your understanding as you experience the results!

I was blown away the first time I realized His activity with my finances. Unforeseen possibilities started happening, unknown events began that stretched my money to new lengths. A job came about that fit both my physical condition and what I enjoyed. There were many opportunities to work extra hours, needed money came from an account I didn't know existed, a free car appeared at my house, and people traded favors that gave way to repairs needed never before affordable.

The favor that the Lord extends to His children has no limits to possibilities. My life drastically changed when I chose to follow Him. Almost seventy years later, I look back and see His hand involved while doing life that I can't even find written about in the bible.

I have my own mental diary of His doings in my life, and you can have yours as well. As you already know, God is no respecter of person, and His grace and mercy are extended to everyone! His favor awaits your choosing, and a blessed life is then just ahead.

CHAPTER SEVEN

Seasons of Life

We are given Scripture telling of times and seasons with various opportunities to make the most of our circumstances. This particular reference covers many selections and what response might need to be implemented at the proper time. Seasons and events take place throughout our entire life. No matter what stage you enter, there will be *seasons and times* as you travel through life needing your participation. Check out this well known Scripture to follow:

Ecclesiastes. 3:1-13:

"For everything there is a season,
    A time for every activity under heaven.
A time to be born and a time to die.
    A time to plant and a time to harvest.
A time to kill and a time to heal.
    A time to tear down and a time to build up.
A time to cry and a time to laugh.
    A time to grieve and a time to dance.
A time to scatter stones and a time to gather stones.

A time to embrace and a time to turn away.
A time to search and a time to quit searching.

A time to keep and a time to throw away.
A time to tear and a time to mend.

A time to be quiet and a time to speak.
A time to love and a time to hate.

A time for war and a time for peace.
What do people really get for all their hard work?

I have seen the burden God has placed on us all.
Yet God has made everything beautiful for its own time.

He has planted eternity in the human heart, but even so, people cannot see the whole scope of God's work from beginning to end.

So I concluded there is nothing better than to be happy and enjoy ourselves as long as we can.

And people should eat and drink and enjoy the fruits of their labor, for these are gifts from God."

In particular, these times and seasons are intended to shape and train us to be aware and cause us to grow in Christlike character while dealing with life. The season of life you are now experiencing is needed to help you become better prepared for what lies ahead. It isn't by chance these seasons occur, because they each have a specific purpose.

Maybe you're waiting for your next promotion in life and are eager to get the show on the road. This is great and always exciting. What I have learned in my life causes me to step back and look at events from a biblical perspective. I find more times than not, I am put on hold while I learn another lesson from the Lord that will better prepare me for that next step.

What am I saying? Maybe I'm not adequately prepared, and the Lord is causing me to deal with specific issues to make me better prepared for the task He has planned in my future. I find that the delay is difficult, and my resistance to wait on the Lord becomes apparent. As I chose to wait on the Lord, I find myself learning from Him what will help me. Being impatient and going ahead of the Lord alone has never worked out well for me. I have learned my impatience, and going it alone did not allow for the best timing.

I have learned many times that we will find the Lord's timing perfect. Our impatience can hinder the desired results if we're not *on time — His time!* It tells me that timing is a great deal more critical than I first thought. Pastor, author, and radio preacher Dr. Charles Swindoll, once said on his radio program: *"Sometimes the timing is as important as the message."* This is so true!

Seasons in life have similarities, just like our weather patterns we experience with each of the four seasons during a calendar year. They are easiest to described as winter, spring, summer, and fall. They each have a specific purpose in timing and correlate with great emphasis on our age and current circumstances. We learn with age and experience that trends and activities will change during our life and must be met by making adjustments. We must then proceed through knowing we will benefit from them to help us achieve the best results that are strengthening and for our future well-being.

> **Winter** — This is the coldest season of the year. It provides rest for basically a three-month period that gives rest and an opportunity for nature to slow down and be prepared to support the next season. A fresh covering of snow, maybe cold rainy crystals that provide moisture for the subsoil and stands in readiness for the next change.

The later years of our aging are considered our winter years because they allow us to slow down and reap from our many seasons in life of harvesting to enjoy our latter days after work becomes too cumbersome. As we age during these years, our preparation will provide less strenuous activity than before and give us more time to experience life from a more comfortable position with ample resources.

> **Spring** — This period is between winter and summer and reveals extreme growth in vegetation. An exuberance of life comes rushing in giving positive results of the winter rest. This spring growth brings evidence that the winter preparation has benefitted greatly and given preparation that becomes advantageous. Springs purpose is preparing for harvest time when the seeds of proper planting take on new growth and reproduce resulting in an abundant harvest.

Spring is a particular time when our growth can expand, and with care and careful attention, will provide a crop that will increase in size and number in readiness for a season of harvest.

> **Summer** — This season brings harvest and the reaping of our crops. Our activities have yielded produce, and as we gather our rewards, we benefit from our labor. The yield has been multiplied during growth, and we are receiving the bounty. The harvest we reap is to supply our needs both now and in the future.

Maybe your retirement preparation will yield an income that will carry you through the years that will cause you to relish life from your storehouse that will supplement the best life possible.

> **Fall** — This season is between summer and winter. Crops, like winter wheat, are planted in the tilled soil and are placed in the earth to begin their several months to root down and become entrenched in the prepared soil. This readiness causes the seed to germinate and grow over the winter months with a

foundational root system anchored into the fertile soil and become readied for plentiful growth during the spring.

We must also consider the many difficulties that can occur during each season and prepare to meet these challenges with wisdom and forethought. For example, a shortage of adequate rain can obviously bring drought that can stifle growth. Too much rain can destroy the seed and cause flooding or even rotting of the seed. Too much or too little of any necessary ingredients can directly affect the growth and the planned harvest yield to follow.

Spring and summer storms can play havoc, especially during harvest season. Hail, wind, lightening, flooding, even insects can reduce crop's productivity and limit its yield. Preparation will help tremendously but does not guarantee avoidance of all the possibilities in these seasons that could lessen the harvest or destroy it altogether.

Every season can have harsh elements that directly affect the potential growth of any living thing. Any harvest season can be filled with several possibilities depending on the conditions, that usually come during this time of year. Sometimes very little harm is experienced while other seasons bring difficulty and hardship, rendering all our efforts to yield little or nothing.

Sometimes the most labor and preparation will not produce the biggest harvest. Variations can be expected, and being ready for whatever lies ahead can enhance our efforts to overcome. It can teach us a great deal about expectations and the reality of life in general.

Life has many similarities as we travel through time, age, events, productivity, hardships, death, birth, failures, successes, and challenges. All these elements are present in each of our lives. They give us reason to call upon the Lord and learn to utilize His help and assistance while traveling on our journey.

All these variables encompass a normal life. Some years are easier than others, while some seem like we can't do anything right. We can earnestly prepare each year, but our efforts can't guarantee that all adverse events will not occur.

At times it doesn't seem fair and probably isn't, but we must not lose hope and move forward. Life, as usual, depending on your particular life span, will include many different events that can and may be experienced.

Because of life's circumstances, we have opportunity to make choices that will assist us in our traveling. It requires a choice on our part to select whether we want the Lord's help or not. Choosing Him doesn't eliminate all of life's troubles, but it will undoubtedly provide a better way to travel and not be alone.

Once we better understand the seasons and stages that life brings, it helps us make better choices and proceed with His help rather than choose to go it alone and take our chances. The selection will depend on us, and the fruit of our actions will yield the crops we plant. Planting good seeds is critical because what grows in your life will manifest during and throughout the entire journey.

Depending on your age and circumstances, each season will build character and cause you to grow and mature as God intends. Each season isn't used to slow you down, but to make you aware that our depending on the Lord can get us through with less difficulty and cause us to learn how to grow and lean on Him for help.

Each season will have different circumstances, but it isn't much different from the Israelites on their journey through the desert. What is around us requires God's help to come out on the other side as a winner. That's the reason for the challenge in the first place. It builds our strength and trust in the Lord to meet the next season of life!

It would not be good to have a harvest season all the time. What about the need to till the soil, plant the seed, and receive the rain, or the warmth of the sunshine to ripen? Preparation is necessary, and if we chose sunshine all the time, what would we have? We would have desert. You know, without all the different seasons, the seeds could not reproduce to make a harvest available!

Just think if you had no rain — that would be a definite problem. Yes, that's when you would experience drought. Seasons have a distinct purpose and learning to function during them and understand the cycle will help us yield a crop during our lifetime. A process of God's origin, plan, and purpose to strengthen us on our journey.

Each of us will experience death in our lifetime. Death is not an easy event, but all things living will eventually die. Ourselves included. That dash between our date of birth will always be followed by the date we die. This fact will take place no matter what. We can't change anything about this factual occurrence. It is 100% true all the time.

We do have a choice of what takes place during that dash between these dates regarding our existence. The dash is what we choose from the options we are given. Our lifetime is summed up with this small symbol (-) when you view a headstone.

The Following is a Poem by Linda Ellis

The Dash

"I read of a man who stood to speak at the funeral of a friend. He referred to the dates on the tombstone from the beginning... to the end.

He noted that first came the date of birth and spoke of the following date with tears, but he said what mattered most of all was the dash between those years.

For that dash represents all the time they spent alive on earth and now only those who loved them know what that little line is worth.

For it matters not, how much we own, the cars... the house... the cash. What matters is how we live and love and how we spend our dash.

So think about this long and hard; are there things you'd like to change? For you never know how much time is left that still can be rearranged.

To be less quick to anger and show appreciation more and love the people in our lives like we've never loved before.

If we treat each other with respect and more often wear a smile… remembering that this special dash might only last a little while.

So when your eulogy is being read, with your life's actions to rehash, would you be proud of the things they say about how you lived your dash?"

When my late wife was buried, I had both our headstones put in place at the same time. After the monument company completed both, I inspected them because I was curious about how they looked.

I was very delighted with the end results, but it looked strange because when I saw my name on a tombstone — yelp! All was completed except my date of death. I wasn't eager to know that information anyway, so leaving it blank was okay. But, it was a different feeling to see my headstone with all the markings that had been selected.

I sometimes think we don't see ourselves as mortal and that our life on earth is unlimited. As long as life is moving forward, why stop and shop for a headstone — right? At least my son and daughter won't have to bother with the details. And, since I've already approved my headstone that won't be a problem either. They certainly won't need to be concerned about how I feel about it. I already told them it's better than I expected.

A note: If I die ten years from now I will have saved money figuring in inflation. That also means I have saved on death as well. Since I'm a woodworker, I should consider building my casket for an additional savings. And you thought older people weren't conservative. I could figure the savings and get me another, larger, and faster drone!

Now — Back to the Book

The more extended time between these dates will add seasons and times with events we will encounter, and our freedom to choose how to act or react is entirely dependent on us. Knowing your choices are so important is critical so that you can select the best possible option for yourself.

Knowing you will die should cause you to choose an option that will suit your choice for an eternal destination. Your destination will come — it's guaranteed! That is a fact that cannot be avoided. I'm prepared now for separation from earth but not very willing just yet.

How you view life and death is essential. It's critical to see these events from a biblical perspective. God's view is factual and does not change, nor is it dependent on how we feel or think. Knowing what the bible tells us will provide an excellent mental picture of the events that will take place and give guidance on how to deal with each. Especially your choice of where to spend Eternity! Remember, your choice is needed to select your destination before life's end.

Since our death is already guaranteed, this fact should alarm us that we need to be ready at any time. If it comes suddenly and unexpectedly, we could be caught off-guard. As we discussed earlier, choosing our desired eternal destination must be made while we are alive.

I know, you didn't choose your parents; you didn't choose to be born, you didn't choose to be alive on planet earth. Nevertheless, you are here. Not a choice we selected but still a reality. So what's the right approach? The right approach is to deal with it — right?

Now, <u>you can</u> select the option made available through the death of Jesus on the cross. Now, <u>you can</u> select an option to where you're headed as a direct result of your decision. Now, by accepting Him, your destination is a personal choice. So know your options and <u>choose for yourself</u>!

Seasonal Effects in Light of Scripture

A season in life does not always mean a specific time of year as we view seasons in our natural world. A season could be from circumstances or events or a particular happening in your life that can take place at any time, and usually, it happens suddenly.

For example, maybe you encounter a person, and when you're around them, you find yourself reacting in a counter-productive way. Perhaps you find yourself angry or upset each time you are together. Maybe a family member or acquaintance is irritating and causes negative feelings and emotions to arise and dominate your actions or responses.

There is an underlying problem in your character, or you would not be reacting in this way. Seeking the Lord to reveal the root problem will cause you to look into your inner-core, which can show the cause. You'll probably discover the Lord is allowing the situation to arise, so this flaw is brought to your attention. This is a sign to pay close attention to His promptings.

Let's say the Lord reveals an area where He wants you to concentrate. He has you turn to Scriptures that deal with this particular issue. Praise God, you're moving in the right direction, and your answer awaits you in following after His scriptural principles found in the bible.

Scripture will give you a godly perspective of your situation and highlights how you could approach this problem. It may not seem logical, and because you have never moved in this direction before it will likely be uncomfortable.

Pursuing a problem from Scripture's perspective may be precisely what is needed to conquer your adverse reaction. This could be your solution to free you from an obstacle standing in the way of spiritual growth your whole life. It maybe a problem that is blocking a better relationship with the Lord, and those you live around.

This kind of occurrence is a phase or area that the Lord wants you to seek Him about, and now is the time. This is a season in your life, and He wants you to deal with it next. Our being changed by the Lord is usually so uncomfortable to our natural self we would rather avoid the solution. The solution will require your participation to accomplish His goal to make the needed changes in your life.

Responding to the Lord will bring healing to that area and a release in your spirit. This release will bring a freedom and peace only the Lord can bring. It will allow His peace to enter your being, and it will remove the root cause in that area He has determined needs fixing. Your positive response to His guidance is intended for you to draw closer to Him.

This kind of change is necessary at this season or specific time in your life, so you may move in His direction and exhibit more Christlike character. Remember, God's timing is always perfect. And, always remember that learning His solution the first time will keep you from repeating the exercise.

Repeats are usually more intense, so learn from me and pass His gentle instruction immediately, so you don't cause Him to turn up the heat. Scripture tells us that correction from the Lord is inevitable because He loves us enough to discipline His children.

The Bible Tells about Discipline from the Lord

> Deuteronomy 8:5:
> *"Think about it: Just as a parent disciplines a child, the Lord your God disciplines you for your own good."*

> Proverbs 3:11:
> *"My child, don't reject the Lord's discipline, and don't be upset when he corrects you."*

> Hebrews 12:6:
> *"For the Lord disciplines those he loves, and he punishes each one he accepts as his child."*

> Hebrews 12:10, 11:
> *"For our earthly fathers* **disciplined** *us for a few years, doing the best they knew how. But God's* **discipline**

is always good for us, so that we might share in his holiness."

*"No **discipline** is enjoyable while it is happening— it's painful! But afterward there will be a peaceful harvest of right living for those who are trained in this way."*

Now, what if you don't choose to move forward as He is directing? Well, this is a common response because we don't want to face the real issue. We may have become comfortable with our natural responses and aren't wanting the needed change. It's our choice to respond to Him, but choosing to refuse His directing — you'd better get ready.

This occurrence is undoubtedly considered a season in our life that is not very enjoyable but has a definite purpose in pointing out a flaw in our character, God wants us to overcome. With God's help, of course. I didn't say growing was easy, but it is necessary to mature and become disciplined God's way during a season like this.

Continuing on our avoidance path because we have somewhat learned to suffer through on our own is not a good idea. Our natural survival tactics, our wall of protection, have been put in place to guard against this kind of situation but will cause God's peace to never come. Our form of protection is not a fix — it's only a temporary solution. Building a wall of protection to protect ourselves ends up blocking out help from the Lord.

As you can surmise, we all are subject to a variety of seasons that can include negative attacks from others, whether we were the cause or not. We find in Scripture that difficulties can come from evil interference, but they can also be our fault. We could be the cause and fully responsible. It could be our reaping of bad seed sown doing our life that has yielded an unwanted crop.

Sometimes we just like to blame the devil for all of our difficult seasons whether he is the cause or not. It's another way to avoid the real issues of life and not take responsibility for the lousy harvest we sowed earlier. Avoidance is not a good way to explain away a root cause for a problem, and neither will it yield a resolve. It could even be discipline from the Lord.

We many times grow accustom to and learn how to protect ourselves against any unwanted situation. Avoidance hasn't worked completely, but we've survived the onslaught that has come against us before, so think we can handle it the next time it appears. We handle the attacks and develop a way to counter the unwanted. We could remove ourselves, as best we can, to guard ourselves and stop or hold at bay this kind of attack.

A very typical maneuver to self-protect, and we all learn this tactic from an early age in life. Most of the attacks are undeserved and certainly unwanted. The attacks carve deep down into our self-worth and cause us to wonder how this could happen. I don't deserve this kind of problem, especially when I didn't cause the problem, to begin with. Nevertheless, a sharp remark or unpleasant situation has invaded your spirit and has left flesh wounds on your soul.

Building a wall of protection is intended to keep away this unwanted situation. But not only does it enclose us, it also places us on the defense and keeps us surrounded by a wall that also entraps us and puts us in isolation and separated from our surroundings. It slowly provides a place of solitary confinement for us. Just think, in prison, solitary confinement is used to punish those who cannot respond to their surroundings with any discipline or self-control.

It becomes a self-made prison that cages us like a wild animal and completely left to ourselves. It guards us from confrontation from all sides but takes away our freedom and encapsulates our emotional state into confinement rather than the intended protection that caused us to build a wall in the first place. The problem is still unsolved and has worsened.

Humankind is notorious when it comes to inflicting pain on another person. It could be their past involved a similar circumstance or that someone was reacting to their issues that were still unresolved. Maybe they were reacting to a deep-seated emotion or feeling they had found no relief from and had grown in the defensive, negative unwanted character and were acting out how they felt.

Unhealed people hurt other people. What they project to others is because of the hurt they have experienced and are feeling. It's like a wave of despair that travels on until the irritation is resolved. It may be from one generation to the next. The irritation must be removed from an individual, or it will continue. We need to break the chain-reaction it causes and follow after the Lord's principles. To break this repeated occurrence requires dealing with the root of the problem — not the symptom.

Now we can see a bigger picture of human nature that desperately needs the Lord to move through these attacks that come from every side. Unhealed people spread this kind of pain their whole life, and if left to itself — it only grows worse over time.

When Jesus came and suffered the excruciating penalty for our sins and died on the cross, He brought a solution to this dilemma. He provided a way to overcome these situations that life brings. He provided a way that may seem strange to humankind but is 100% effective. Not partial, but entirely above anything the world has to offer. A solution and release from areas of despair that have so enormously affected our lives.

The Lord knows what kind of world we're born into and how to deal with our many issues. He understands humanity can be brutal because He has experienced their cruelty as He journeyed to His crucifixion and death on the cross. Humanity became so terrible, at one point in history, He flooded the world to remove the filth and evil that prevailed at that time.

If Noah hadn't been willing or available, God's removal of evil from the earth might have removed our existence in the future. Whew! But, here we are, and now we have a solution, Christ, that can help us get beyond ourselves because of the Holy Spirit He sent to empower us if we will but follow His leading and directions!

The 'nature' of things without the Lord will evolve into a total mess. It proved out once before, and we can read about it (Genesis

6:5-7). The Lord knows our inability and lack of power to overcome sin and provided a means to cover and overcome sin's penalty. He also provided His help to plow through these seasons and times of trials during our lives!

Knowing what to do to rise above your difficulties is crucial. It boils down to a choice, once again, and believers are the only ones that can follow a godly path. It isn't left up to chance — it's left up to us to choose purposely. We do have God's principles available to eliminate past hurts.

We don't get to choose the circumstances or the location, or parents, or culture or where God places us, but we do get to decide how to rise above all that is presented. He has seen to that by sending Christ. Our Lord has provided the wisdom, principles, and power to overcome any season, circumstance, storm, difficulty, climate, etc., we face in life.

I believe we are born precisely where the Lord wants us and that our circumstances and challenges in life are determined explicitly for us personally. God knows us so well that our exact location (including the time period) is specific so that the circumstances will play a significant part in our coming back to Him by choice.

No accidents, no roulette choices, not the flip of a coin, but exactness and a precise location so that we will react and choose to follow Him. The verse we know so well is:

John 3:16:
"For God so loved the world that He gave His only begotten Son, that whoever believes in Him should not perish but have everlasting life." (NKJV)

God knows our personalities, and He knows what affects us the most, and He places us in an environment that will best cause us to respond willingly, back to Him, so we will choose Him and return saved for all eternity.

Why? So we will choose Him over all else and that He will have a willing vessel responsive to the bible He gave us. He is waiting to supply our every need in life. He wants us willing and available to ensure our survival and utilize His strength to overcome all in our path. His plan includes His help to rise above all that we encounter.

If we choose to do life on our own, we choose the most challenging path. It will lead you on a journey of greatest difficulty and a continued trail to develop a hardness that directly affects your heart. Look at the parable found in Matthew chapter 13:1-23:

Parable of the Farmer Scattering Seed

> *"Later that same day Jesus left the house and sat beside the lake. A large crowd soon gathered around him, so he got into a boat. Then he sat there and taught as the people stood on the shore."*
>
> *"He told many stories in the form of parables, such as this one: 'Listen! A farmer went out to plant some seeds. As he scattered them across his field, some seeds fell on a footpath, and the birds came and ate them.'"*
>
> *"Other seeds fell on shallow soil with underlying rock. The seeds sprouted quickly because the soil was shallow. But the plants soon wilted under the hot sun, and since they didn't have deep roots, they died."*
>
> *"Other seeds fell among thorns that grew up and choked out the tender plants. Still other seeds fell on fertile soil, and they produced a crop that was thirty, sixty, and even a hundred times as much as had been planted!"*
>
> *"Anyone with ears to hear should listen and understand." His disciples came and asked him, "Why do you use parables when you talk to the people?" He replied, "You are permitted to understand the secrets of the Kingdom of Heaven, but others are not."*
>
> *"To those who listen to my teaching, more understanding will be given, and they will have an abundance of knowledge. But for those who are not*

listening, even what little understanding they have will be taken away from them."

"That is why I use these parables, For they look, but they don't really see. They hear, but they don't really listen or understand."

"This fulfills the prophecy of Isaiah that says, 'When you hear what I say, you will not understand. When you see what I do, you will not comprehend."

"For the hearts of these people are hardened, and their ears cannot hear, and they have closed their eyes— so their eyes cannot see, and their ears cannot hear, and their hearts cannot understand, and they cannot turn to me and let me heal them."

"But blessed are your eyes, because they see; and your ears, because they hear. I tell you the truth, many prophets and righteous people longed to see what you see, but they didn't see it. And they longed to hear what you hear, but they didn't hear it."

"Now listen to the explanation of the parable about the farmer planting seeds: The seed that fell on the footpath represents those who hear the message about the Kingdom and don't understand it. Then the evil one comes and snatches away the seed that was planted in their hearts."

"The seed on the rocky soil represents those who hear the message and immediately receive it with joy. But since they don't have deep roots, they don't last long. They fall away as soon as they have problems or are persecuted for believing God's word."

"The seed that fell among the thorns represents those who hear God's word, but all too quickly the message is crowded out by the worries of this life and the lure of wealth, so no fruit is produced."

"The seed that fell on good soil represents those who truly hear and understand God's word and produce

a harvest of thirty, sixty, or even a hundred times as
much as had been planted!"

What do you see from this Scripture as it relates to the soil conditions and what you can expect? This parable provides us with a perspective that is both godly and easy to understand from the natural realm that we live.

Its application is to help us better understanding our spiritual condition based on the workings of the surroundings in which we each live. It gives a word photograph and how viewing the natural compares with the spiritual.

We are given four different soil conditions and how each is responsive to being seeded and exactly what we can expect.

The First Soil Condition

> *"Listen! A farmer went out to plant some seeds. As he*
> *scattered them across his field, some seeds fell on a*
> *footpath, and the birds came and ate them."*

What? Wasted seed? No, the farmer (God) <u>equally distributed</u> the seeds over the existing soil, but because the soil was hard, the seed could not penetrate the surface. So, what happened? The good seed remained on the surface and was taken away and utilized elsewhere instead of its original purpose.

What Do We Learn From This?

> Jeremiah 4:3:
> *"This is what the Lord says to the people of Judah and*
> *Jerusalem: 'Plow up the hard ground of your hearts! Do*
> *not waste your good seed among thorns.'"*

He is saying to us beware of your hearts condition. When God's Word is sown it cannot take root in a hard heart. What was the original purpose? To take root and grow and reproduce itself. For these seeds were to take root and reveal the package of Salvation that God offers in Jesus Christ. Our Passover Lamb to enter Stage 4.

What Does Scripture tell us About being Hard Hearted?

Hosea 10:12:
I said, 'Plant the good seeds of righteousness, and you will harvest a crop of love. Plow up the hard ground of your hearts, for now is the time to seek the Lord, that he may come and shower righteousness upon you.'

The Second Soil Condition

"Other seeds fell on shallow soil with underlying rock. The seeds sprouted quickly because the soil was shallow. But the plants soon wilted under the hot sun, and since they didn't have deep roots, they died."

This soil was not too hard on the surface, but it had no depth for the seed to take root and survive the natural elements that normally came during the season. As a result of this shallow soil condition, it was soft enough on top but was still resistant to reproducing anything fruitful because of the hardness just below the surface.

Surface softness accompanied by hardened subsoil does not produce godly fruit. It produces nothing lasting of the Lord's planting and does not allow for growth. Looking good on the outside surface while being self-sufficient on the inside yields no eternal gain.

Luke 8:12:
"The seeds that fell on the footpath represent those who hear the message, only to have the devil come and take it away from their hearts and prevent them from believing and being saved."

James 1:21:
"So get rid of all the filth and evil in your lives, and humbly accept the word God has planted in your hearts, for it has the power to save your souls."

The Third Soil Condition

"Other seeds fell among thorns that grew up and choked out the tender plants."

1 John 5:21:
"Dear children, keep away from anything that might take God's place in your hearts."

What kind of soil was this? It was good soil (soft—tilled) that was receptive to the seeds and allowed the seed to take root. The problem was that as the seeds grew, it also received 'other seed,' and they were also allowed to grow.

Both kind of seed, the bad and the good seed, remained together. Then, the bad seed outgrew the good seed and overshadowed the good seed. This caused the good seed to be smothered out before it had time to reproduce its kind, and a very lean harvest was the result.

Little to no return from the good seed, but the soil was not the problem. What was the problem? The seeds of desire, greed, earthly goods were attended to rather than the good seeds of spiritual fruit. What was the reason for this happening? Attention was directed toward the bad seeds and the good seeds were neglected.

The bad seeds were cared for most, while the good seeds were ignored. The good seeds did not grow while the bad seeds were attended to instead. Because the seeds being fed grew more rapidly, which is always the case, it eliminated the good seeds from receiving the Sonshine and nourishment necessary for ultimate growth. Staying busy isn't a good barometer of success, nor is it a trait that draws us closer to the Lord.

God's greatest concern isn't about what you're doing because He is looking to the heart of man to determine what he is really like. The condition of our heart, above all else, is what God sees and desires for us to grow us forward in His care.

> Matthew 23:28:
> *"Outwardly you look like righteous people, but inwardly your hearts are filled with hypocrisy and lawlessness."*

> Jeremiah 7:24:
> *"But my people would not listen to me. They kept doing whatever they wanted, following the stubborn desires of their evil hearts. They went backward instead of forward."*

This is because you allow other interests to dominate your choices, and they crowd out the good seeds God has planted to take root. You have given room for the cares of this world to take control and lead your interests rather than concentrate on the things of the Lord as He had intended.

> Romans 8:27:
> *"And the Father who knows all hearts knows what the Spirit is saying, for the Spirit pleads for us believers in harmony with God's own will."*

> 2 Thessalonians 3:5:
> *"May the Lord lead your hearts into a full understanding and expression of the love of God and the patient endurance that comes from Christ."*

The Fourth Soil Condition

> *"Still other seeds fell on fertile soil, and they produced a crop that was thirty, sixty, and even a hundred times as much as had been planted! Anyone with ears to hear should listen and understand."*

We should listen carefully to what the Lord is saying from this parable. Reading it and then applying what is says is necessary to experience the fullness of wisdom intended. It reveals a great deal about our heart's condition and how it will grow and expand. It gives us reason to examine ourselves in light of God's Word and to focus on Him.

A red light should be flashing in our minds, giving us a reason for concern when evaluating the condition of our heart. Our heart's condition is critical in the eyes of the Lord and is what He sees when looking at our soul!

Invite Him in and Let His Holy Spirit take Residence

> 2 Corinthians 1:22:
> *"And he has identified us as his own by placing the Holy Spirit in our hearts as the first installment that guarantees everything he has promised us."*

> Ephesians 3:17:
> *"Then Christ will make his home in your hearts as you trust in him. Your roots will grow down into God's love and keep you strong."*

The Lord is good to express Himself, as He explains in the Book of Matthew chapter 13, to the disciples the parable of the Farmer Scattering Seed. Also read on in verses 14 through 23 and see for yourself God's clarity. As you read, stop for a moment to listen, not just hear, what is being said and take it to heart knowing this kind of wisdom — only the Lord can give.

> Matthew 13:11-13:
> *He replied, "You are permitted to understand the secrets of the Kingdom of Heaven, but others are not."*
> *"To those who listen to my teaching, more understanding will be given, and they will have an abundance of knowledge. But for those who are not*

listening, even what little understanding they have will be taken away from them."

"That is why I use these parables, for they look, but they don't really see. They hear, but they don't really listen or understand."

Refuse Satan's Alternative and Obey God's Word

Ephesians 2:2:
"You used to live in sin, just like the rest of the world, obeying the devil—the commander of the powers in the unseen world. He is the spirit at work in the hearts of those who refuse to obey God."

Stop making Excuses for Disobedience

Proverbs 24:12:
"Don't excuse yourself by saying, 'Look, we didn't know.' For God understands all hearts, and he sees you. He who guards your soul knows you knew. He will repay all people as their actions deserve."

Hebrews 3:8:
"Don't harden your hearts as Israel did when they rebelled, when they tested me in the wilderness."

The Lord sees all and is aware of our precise heart condition and is not impressed with the outward expressions provided in our attempts to win favor with Him. He is a God that discerns from where the actions originate. Thinking otherwise is foolish.

The Religion of Man

Matthew 15:8:
"These people honor me with their lips, but their hearts are far from me."

An Equal Opportunity God — by Faith

> Acts 15:9:
> *"He made no distinction between us (Gentile) and them (Jew), for he cleansed their hearts through faith."*

Self Evident

> 2 Corinthians 4:7:
> *"We now have this light shining in our hearts, but we ourselves are like fragile clay jars containing this great treasure. This makes it clear that our great power is from God, not from ourselves."*

God is our Guardian

> Philippians 4:7:
> *"Then you will experience God's peace, which exceeds anything we can understand. His peace will guard your hearts and minds as you live in Christ Jesus."*

Viewing this parable in Scripture and using it as a measuring stick and the principles of nature is revealing. The facts regarding spiritual things is crucial to our understanding and enlightenment. Its message supersedes the limits of time and the culture we live in.

This message is essential to understanding our heart condition and how our lives can be changed should we allow the Lord to enter. He desires that we would hear His voice and follow His guidance by faith!

When you realize that lasting change in our heart condition is only available through the Lord, you come to a very significant scriptural fact. Look at the Book of Romans and you will obtain greater wisdom from the Lord.

Romans 2:29:

"No, a true Jew is one whose heart is right with God. And true circumcision is not merely obeying the letter of the law; rather, it is a change of heart produced by the Spirit. And a person with a changed heart seeks praise from God, not from people."

Who is a True Believer?

A true believer is one who's heart is right with God. So what is true circumcision? Not a fleshly cutting away of skin, but a change of heart only the Holy Spirit can do.

A changed heart seeks fellowship with God, and wants to please God, and becomes unconcerned about what other people think. A change from God is radical and completely turns us away from our narrow and natural viewpoint of life. It provides a whole new approach to living and learning and coming into a relationship with our Creator.

This new change gives us power through obedience to His Word that provides us the opportunity to sail through life with a completely different set of directions. This change gives us avenues to approach life utilizing God's power, His Holy Spirit, that is living in us once we accept His offer of Salvation.

❧

CHAPTER EIGHT

What is Pneuma Hagion?

Now, let me share a nugget of gold with you that has exhilarated me to a place I did not know existed for most of my life. This new biblical understanding began as I started to write this book.

I will now insert a definition taken from related information and put it precisely into a summation of how, if possible, to explain this facet of the Holy Spirit and His doings on earth today.

Pneuma —The root pneu forms the Greek word pneuma, meaning "spirit air" or "breath of life." It is regularly translated as "spirit" or "soul".

This meaning can be thought of as the breath of God as viewed generally throughout its ancient Greek origin. When God 'breathed' into man, life became input as a result.

Genesis 2:7: "Then the Lord God formed the man from the dust of the ground. He breathed the breath of life into the man's nostrils, and the man became a living person."

Hagion — This Greek word took me on an adventure way beyond my pay grade, which provided pages and pages of references and locations, but I believe it can be translated as "holy". This meaning appears throughout my readings and is the best definition I could find. Simple yes — but Divine in application and meaning!

Now, when Pneuma (spirit air or breath of life) is paired with hagion, ("holy"), it becomes pneuma hagion, translated as "Holy Spirit" or "Holy Ghost." The Holy Spirit of God has been sent by Jesus to give us the Comforter, which is the Spirit of God living inside of us once we accept Him by faith for our salvation.

As you already know, salvation is only part of God's dynamics, which provides us with the knowledge of the heart of God in a spiritual partnership as He breathes His Spirit into the believer.

When we say the Holy Bible is "inspired of God," did you know we are actually emphasizing the Person (the Holy Ghost) who gave it to us? Wow! We are saying God Himself has provided a way to live in each of us who believe.

The indwelling of the Holy Spirit of God projects our possibilities in existence way beyond the abilities of humankind. It ushers us into the spiritual realm, with benefits superseding our capabilities. At the same time, it provided the opportunity to soar above this realm of physical reality while we still live in our earthly bodies.

> John 3:6:
> *"Humans can reproduce only human life, but the Holy Spirit gives birth to <u>spiritual life</u>. The Holy Spirit gives birth to your spiritual life once you accept Christ and believe on Him."*

There is more to living as you learn to experience His presence and fellowship with Him! The Holy Spirit that lives inside of you will give birth to His presence as you learn to release Him and come before the Lord with clean hands and a pure heart (1 Timothy 1:5). This receiving of His presence begins a spiritual walk like no other.

Many advantages become real in our lives when we grow and learn how to fellowship with the Lord. It is an ongoing relationship, and His desire is that we will experience Him and visit often. How? By pursuing Him with our best efforts and to communicate with Him each day. Our willingness to follow His leading to our best abilities sets our path toward Him and puts Him first in our life!

STAGE 6

Stage 6 is where the Lord desires for us to arrive in life. And, that is His continued presence within that stirs our desires, guides our every emotion and feelings, and fills our spirit with a sense of God that far surpasses our natural thinking and estimation with endless possibilities. It is a stage that produces His fruit in our lives that maximize the works He intends for each believer. I see this as life in the physical realm to the extent of His desires for all humanity!

I'm certainly not an expert on entering Stage 6, but I have sampled it several times with what seems to me to be an out-of-the-body probability to a degree. I want to remain in God's presence, but know I'm still in my earthly body the whole time.

I would compare it to entering a quiet place with no conscience awareness of temperature, soft lighting with a sense of peace inside that calms me down and settles my spirit, allowing me to relax and yearn for more. Sometimes I become overwhelmed in my spirit and softly cry because it is so peaceful. I find comfort and peace beyond any human experience.

I find my daily functions become more effortless, and my ability to be more productive is enhanced, and my becoming tired does not enter into what I'm doing. Just everyday functions are less challenging to accomplish what the Lord has expressed on you that day. This stage brings a whole new dimension in serving Him.

This continued awareness of His Holy Spirit enhances my feelings for Him and makes Him more real. I feel like I've breached a gap between the physical and the spiritual that explains a part of the love inside that surpasses mine to a place I never knew existed before He came into my life.

I have found that discernment is elevated to a level that must be guarded and discussed only with the Lord. It brings with it insight and understanding meant for spiritual observation and acquired sensitivity exceeding the limits found in no other place.

It causes compassion to accelerate and requires immediate prayer to satisfy its presence and unctions. Heartache and awareness of sorrow for others will heighten with a compelling urgency to comfort a person in spiritual conditions of danger that seem to be real in thought.

There is always an awareness that you cannot help in situations, and the only option is to immediately call upon the Lord. Your thoughts are full of areas that the Lord wants you to pray for and about. Your sensitivity to the Holy Spirit continues to grow in-depth and in a deeper loving relationship and longing for His presence.

There are days when you are not as sensitive, cause you to long for His presents and companionship. These are times you feel somewhat lost and alone. Learning more about yourself brings a better understanding of why, and will cause you to be more aware of your attitudes and habits that the Lord would like to let Him eliminate in your character.

Events in your life that once caused you despair take on much less intensity, and your ability to maintain peace is pleasant and refreshing. Things that used to bring dismay and discomfort will almost be forgotten, and your self-control becomes almost commonplace.

Your desires continue to change, and new adventures with the Lord become more commonplace in your life. Moments of inspired understanding spring from reading His Word. It may even be a very familiar verse that evolves into a whole new meaning never before observed or applied.

As the Lord continually becomes more real in your life, the familiarity with His Word is transformed into a bigger picture and reasons for His involvement with humankind and what sending His Son entailed in saving us from ourselves trying to run our own lives.

His love for humanity is amazing, and His plan of grace during this lifetime has been extended to the end of time as we read in Revelation. The Lord will go to extreme measures to save everyone that will call on His name. He does not want anyone to be lost into eternity and experience Eternal damnation.

This Stage 6 brings us to a better understanding of God, His Son, and the power of His Holy Spirit — which has been sent for the very purpose of getting us through now and into eternity experiencing Him all along the way.

His plan for us is so amazing and complete. His intent couldn't be better, and since He has provided everything needed to travel from here into Eternity with Him — well, the gifts God provided through Jesus Christ are just what we need to rise above and soar with Him, both now and forever more.

Let Today be…

The End

of

Choosing to live life your way only

and let it be…

The Beginning

of

Living life as God intended

In fellowship with the Holy Spirit

CHAPTER NINE

What Can Heaven be Like?

STAGE 7

> Stage 7 is our final resting place for a believer and the Eternal destination we all should desire. Once we leave our earthly body and our soul and spirit go to be in the presence of the Lord, our earthly journey is complete, and our endless time in Eternity begins. A final place of residence that will put us together with the Lord forever.

We arrive at our chosen destination when life on earth ends. No one is for certain what that destination will be exactly like, but from the several glimpses we are given in Scriptures will give us some idea.

A Place has been Built for each of Us

> John 14:2:
> *"In My Father's house are many mansions; if it were not so, I would have told you. I go to prepare a place for you."*

According to Webster's Dictionary, this could be an apartment within a mansion, even a manor house. But, God has made each believer a *place* in eternity to reside He calls a mansion. Your heavenly Father has prepared a heavenly residence that will be waiting for each of us.

Your eternal retirement home will be waiting when you depart this earth. This home is another perk that accompanies our Salvation Package when it's time to go home and spend eternity with God. This is the beginning of an everlasting life that will be more than we can imagine.

What Does the Bible Say about Heaven

The bible offers us glimpses into heaven with imagery to give us a hint of what we may encounter when we arrive. The following Scriptures provide that snapshot:

> Acts 7:55,56:
> *"But Stephen, full of the Holy Spirit, gazed steadily into heaven and saw the glory of God, and he saw Jesus standing in the place of honor at God's right hand. And he told them, 'Look, I see the heavens opened and the Son of Man standing in the place of honor at God's right hand!'"*

This snapshot of heaven was given by Stephen when he was being stoned to death. The Jewish council stoned him after his presentation in response to the high priest. They were in denial of the accusations Stephen spoke about them, and stoning was the punishment (Acts 7:1-53).

> Revelation 4:2-6:
> *"And instantly I was in the Spirit, and I saw a throne in heaven and someone sitting on it."*
> *"One sitting on the throne was as brilliant as gemstones—like jasper and carnelian. And the glow of an emerald circled his throne like a rainbow."*

"Twenty-four thrones surrounded him, and twenty-four elders sat on them. They were all clothed in white and had gold crowns on their heads."

"From the throne came flashes of lightning and the rumble of thunder. And in front of the throne were seven torches with burning flames. This is the sevenfold Spirit of God."

"In front of the throne was a shiny sea of glass, sparkling like crystal."

The revelation above was recorded in the New Testament, as described by the disciple John in a vision. John was on the isle of Patmos as he received this vision of the future from the Lord. We see a brilliance of light reflecting from God's throne with images of worshiping spectators and a sea of believers looking on.

Look at Scripture taken from the Old Testament, revealing more of heaven and what it must look like through man's eyes. The prophet Ezekiel gives a descriptive snapshot as the Lord appears to him in a vision. Read Ezekiel 1:1-28 and listen to what the prophet Ezekiel reveals.

Daniel 7:9,10:
"I watched as thrones were put in place and the Ancient One sat down to judge. His clothing was as white as snow, his hair like purest wool. He sat on a fiery throne with wheels of blazing fire, and a river of fire was pouring out, flowing from his presence. Millions of angels ministered to him; many millions stood to attend him. Then the court began its session, and the books were opened."

Millions upon millions were before the Lord as He sat before them in heaven. Other Scriptures provide a word picture of heaven, as found in Psalm 96:6 and Revelation 21:21.

We see that the streets are paved with gold; God's presence is glorious (Revelation 21:10-27). In heaven, we see the city of God, which has 12 foundations, each made of different precious stones. On each foundation, we see written the names of the twelve apostles. There are 12 gates — each is a single pearl with a name for each of the 12 tribes of Israel.

The streets are made of pure gold are so pure they are transparent. Through the city flows the river of life that is lined with trees that bear a different type of fruit each month, and the trees have leaves that provide healing for the nations.

We see in Revelation 22:5 that there is no need for the sun or moon because all light comes from the Lord. Illumination beyond anything we have ever seen before. We are given only a glimpse because heaven will be more glorious than we can imagine (1 Corinthians 2:9).

In addition to what is visible, we can add to heaven's description as a place without sorrow, pain, or tears (Revelation 21:4). Death is no longer present and can never separate us from a loved one again (Revelation 20:6). There will be no sickness, no doubt or fear, and no sin will be present. No longer will we experience anything, but the goodness and blessings of God and His presence will be continual. This is our description of heaven, as we see written in the bible. There is more to follow after death on earth. Your will experience much more on arrival where your heavenly home is awaiting you!

When we look at the Temple of God that Moses built on earth, we can visualize a layout as God instructed Moses because the patterned reflected God's heavenly location. The Temple on earth was to reveal God's design reflecting the real city in heaven with valuable replicas from earthly treasures made of gold and silver.

Remember the earthly front of the later Temple Solomon had constructed? It had entrance doors overlaid with gold and the doors for the Holy of Holies' entrance. Tons of gold was used by Solomon when constructing the Temple. The queen of Sheba gave King Solomon a gift of 9,000 pounds of gold and significant quantities of spices and precious jewels (I Kings 10:10).

The collecting of gold appears plentiful when reading just in I Kings chapters 9 and 10. In just a few Scriptures, I counted 25 tons of gold in gifts, and King Solomon received 25 tons of gold each year in preparation for building the Temple. This is what I call a gold rush.

We hear of stories of what heaven is like, but what the bible tells us is all we know for sure. Yes, folks have told stories about their near-death experiences with tales of what they saw, but we can only imagine from what they tell us in visualizing what lies ahead.

I read in 1 Corinthians 2:9 that we can't even imagine how heaven will appear. Still, with all the stories and biblical descriptions available today, I certainly can fantasize for myself without really knowing for certain. I am excited to view it one day, but I don't want to rush the eternal visit just yet. I want to live a full life on earth before my journey home to forever land.

Our understanding is limited regarding heaven, but we believe it is a real place prepared by God and where we will live through Eternity with Him (John 14:1-3). Jesus refers to heaven as a place where His Father lives and where Jesus will spend Eternity. When we look into Revelation chapter 21, we can see a vast city with many people present.

Jesus told the believing thief on the Cross that his choice would take him to dwell in paradise with Him. Heaven was their destination. A designated location, according to Luke chapter 23, verse 43. A place where a believer will be located when their earthly journey ends.

Scripture is good to provide references that are facts about heaven from which we can draw our own conclusion. Some bible references I found are:

- Heaven is referred to as Paradise — Luke 23:43.
- Jesus calls it His Fathers house — John 14:1-3.
- Where Jesus is today at His Father's right hand — Acts 1:11.
- Where Christians will go once they die — Philippians 1:21-23.
- Heaven is a city that God designed and built — Hebrews 11:10.

- The place where God dwells — Deut. 26:15; 1 Kings 8:49; Psalm 33:13; Jeremiah 25:30.
- God speaks from heaven — 1 Samuel 7:10.
- God is the LORD of Heaven's Armies — 2 Samuel 7:26.
- God hears from heaven where He lives — 2 Chronicles 6:21, 23, 25, 27, 30, 33, 35, 39.
- God operates from His heavenly home — Psalm 20:6; 53:2; 82:11; 103:19; Ecclesiastes 5:2.
- Heaven is God's throne — Matthew 5:34.
- Heaven is a city with many people — Revelation, chapter 21

In Hebrews, we read about what the gospel (Good News) has accomplished for us. We learn about the heavenly city, the place of many angels, and who is present before the Lord.

> Hebrews 12:22-24:
> *"But you have come to Mount Zion, to the heavenly Jerusalem, the city of the living God. You have come to thousands upon thousands of angels in joyful assembly, to the church of the firstborn, whose names are written in heaven. You have come to God, the judge of all men, to the spirits of righteous men made perfect, to Jesus the mediator of a new covenant, and to the sprinkled blood that speaks a better word than the blood of Abel."*

The Hebrew Scripture provides many mental snapshots of what we are told about heaven. We can ascertain a portion of what is going on there. Having our name in the Book of Life places us among the names written in heaven and lets us know that we will spend eternity with the LORD. Those *spirits of righteous men made perfect* lets us know that if we who have accepted Jesus as our Savior are the *men made perfect* in Christ and will be part of this biblical description from Hebrews.

Our departure from earth upon death, for a believer, will cause us to directly go into the presence of the Lord according to Scripture.

Take a look at the following and see how the apostle Paul explains our earth body and how we take on a spiritual body when our physical death on earth comes:

> 2 Corinthians 5:5-8:
> *"For we know that when this earthly tent we live in is taken down (that is, when we die and leave this earthly body), we will have a house in heaven, an eternal body made for us by God himself and not by human hands."*
>
> *"We grow weary in our present bodies, and we long to put on our heavenly bodies like new clothing. For we will put on heavenly bodies; <u>we will not be spirits without bodies</u>."*
>
> *"While we live in these earthly bodies, we groan and sigh, but it's not that we want to die and get rid of these bodies that clothe us. Rather, we want to put on our new bodies so that these dying bodies will be swallowed up by life. God himself has prepared us for this, and as a guarantee he has given us his Holy Spirit."*
>
> *"So we are always confident, even though we know that as long as we live in these bodies we are not at home with the Lord. For we live by believing and not by seeing. Yes, we are fully confident, and we would rather be away from these earthly bodies, for then we will be at home with the Lord."*

I really like this scriptural picture written for us to understand better the change we will experience once we physically die and pass on into eternity. I believe our faith in the Lord is so rewarding that we are given a glimpse to see into our future as believers. A glimpse that brings hope and encouragement and to know some of what lies ahead in Stage 7.

Our knowing this earthly life is not the end but will release us into a portal into eternity. There we will be welcomed, and Christ's presence will always be experienced. There we will exist without all the earthly circumstances to dampen our joy or hinder our walk with Him.

Heaven is a city of hope that is directly in our future once our earthly journey ends. Heaven has been prepared for us ahead of our death. Our future appears to be so glorious. But, since we aren't able to imagine all that is in store for us there — we will have to wait and see. Heaven will be better than we can even imagine — Wow!

A few years ago, my mother ask me to tell her what it was like to die and go to heaven. She wanted to know, thinking it would give her an idea of what the trip might entail and what heaven would be like. When I told her I didn't know, she was somewhat irritated with my response.

I told her I did not know the answer to her question. I ask her why she thought I would know something like this? I hadn't died before or had a near-death experience. She said that since I read the bible so much, I should have an answer for her. I told her that after she made the trip herself, to let me know what it was like so I could have (almost) firsthand knowledge.

That suggestion wasn't very popular, either. So, since our visit, she has passed away making the trip unknowing. She has not written and let me know how the journey went, and I'm still not anymore informed or knowledgeable about the answer to her question than I was before.

Wouldn't you think my own mother would have just let me know? Nope — I haven't heard a word since she left and don't expect to either. She's probably forgotten all about our visit and enjoying her new location. Besides, she was tired of being old and was ready for a change. And, a change was just what she got!

If I could guess, she might be rearranging a few of the decorations in her mansion and making a few new decorations herself because she was so creative. I'm sure she's keeping the place spotless and clean, rearranging the furniture (if there is any) and telling my dad to be sure and take off his shoes before entering — just in case there's grass clippings on his feet. Of course, that will depend on whatever one wears with their new spiritual body and if mowing is even necessary.

Oh yes, and if she could — a small, 7 pound, full of life white Chihuahua named Cha-Cha would be her dog of choice. Just before she passed away, she was talking about maybe seeing her dog when she arrived and wouldn't that be great!

So, if animals are in heaven, and I think they are (Isaiah 11:6-9), we can enjoy their presence and have a creation of God's to bring companionship even better than we experienced while living on earth. But, since we can't imagine exactly what heaven is like — it looks to me like we'll just have to wait and see for ourselves.

A Final Thought about Heaven

Like I said before, in Chapter 2, a non-believer will not experience this heavenly dimension in the afterlife called Eternity. Their choice for eternity will be based on whether they accepted the Salvation Package Jesus offered or not. Throughout their life, this choice was available in Stage 2 but will catapult them to Stage 3 upon their physical death if they have refused Christ.

These two choices make up what's available in the here and now — Stage 2. Before life ends (in the here and now), the decision must be made to choose where to spend Eternity. So — don't forget your options and what they each will yield.

Choose with the knowledge given in Scriptures and select your destination. There are no other selections available, and we cannot alter or fudge our entrance into eternity by any other means or way. Conditions such as this may not be to our liking and may not reflect our natural desires, but they do provide an avenue by selection, and we must make the choice for ourselves!

CHAPTER TEN

Why is Life so Difficult?

Life is tough, but without the Lord's help, it is even more difficult. Our limited human condition has a great need for the Lord's help. Difficulties are a part of living but can be used for our learning and benefit us greatly. Our perspective in viewing all challenges as unfavorable will soon be dashed once we learn from them by asking for God's help. Learning from the lessons they teach is our beginning on the road to success.

When I left home after high school and went directly to college, I could hardly wait to get out from under my parents stern hand. Even though I had ignored several essential details — I was eager to get started. I was like a bullet that shot out the front door catapulted into the future. This rapid departure included an attitude that my knowledge about everything would get me immediately where I wanted to go.

As you might guess, there was a lot out there I never even thought about and certainly hadn't experienced or knew how to handle. Much of my education was learned the hard way, which seems to be the norm with many teenagers. I wasn't an exception, even though I was sure at the time I was.

Now fifty-some years later, I can see backward much better than I saw forward. Isn't it amazing how our viewpoint can change with the many lessons life brings across our path. I always knew the Lord, but utilizing His instructions and the Holy Spirit's power was unknown to me back then. I thought determination, will-power, and hard work would take me anywhere.

I thought you had to discipline yourself and do what was right, and that was all there was to it. Trying to solve my problems became much easier when I learned to call upon the Lord and ask for His help. When I found what I needed to apply to my circumstances, it brought great relief and a greater trust in the Lord than ever.

I grew, and I got to see Him work with the different issues because I didn't know a solution or even what to look for in the beginning. When looking back, I marvel at how He resolved the many problems that were waiting for me in my future. My continued growth and His presence became real to my doubting mind.

Most of the time, I was uncertain how His ways could possibly work, but they did. Some problems took years to work out, and the result was always more than I expected possible. Besides, His guidance was not the way I would have handled the matter to resolve the problem.

College was educational, but the school of hard knocks had a much more meaningful schedule accompanied by a rigorous curriculum that I never thought existed. The unofficial school of learning provides one to learn from their mistakes and successes rather than learn about life and apply scriptural principles. And, plenty of mistakes became apparent to me as I ventured forward in my pursuit of happiness and success.

Getting married and the responsibilities that accompanied this relationship were very challenging. I started with a wife with two children and got a crash course in parenting. It was a great adventure for me, and them too, but I loved being a father and I loved the three of them more than I thought was possible. Marriage and parenting were another one of those learning times with the Lord that takes years to realize what He accomplished in changing me into a better person.

I didn't think I was all that bad, but it proved out I wasn't doing near as well as I thought. I thought I had it all together, but there existed such a gap from where the Lord wanted me, and where I was; it took years to remodel what I thought was an okay life. Surprise — significant changes were necessary, and with such a stubborn person, well, the Lord's patience was required, as well as, His loving persistence.

His grace and mercy have been evident throughout my lifetime. I am very grateful for His hand on my life. I needed Him to lead me down the path set for me before I was born. I've been a rascal a few times in my life and very set on doing things my way. I never really trusted anybody for help growing up. So I determined early on, I could do much better on my own.

I see other cultures that instill knowledge to their children, that causes them to watch and listen to what they are being told. I think we in America provide so many different avenues to learn from that it is easy to bypass the essentials and wander off track.

It seems we provide too many choices and give too much to our children so early in life that their concept of life can slip toward entitlement privileges. Learning and maintaining a standard of morals acceptable to biblical standards will save a tremendous amount of consequences that could be avoided if practiced.

Learning to honor our elders and parents has slipped to a much lower standard than God recommends. Being responsible for our actions and learning that consequences follow if you break the law has slid in importance to our current living standards. In our society today, it seems more acceptable to blame others rather than be responsible for our own actions.

Our Worldly Thinking Can Harm the Outcome

When I hear that a church teaches illegal immigrants how to avoid the law and remain in America, I am saddened of where we will end up if we teach others to break the law and that it's okay, especially when it is a church doing the teaching.

When I look at our government, I become grievous to learn we have veered away from our God-given Constitution and have politicians who want our government replaced with socialism. I think what has happened to our commonsense and logical thinking, and why have we left our God-given foundation of fundamentals and beliefs?

The statements I hear on television and read about on the news boggle my mind to think people in power believe all this nonsense? Where have I been to let the country and freedom I fought for in Vietnam slide into a trench of socialistic leftist who want to override our Constitution then accuse another person for doing this when they are the ones who have veered off track? I was taught this was 'the pot calling the kettle black.' What's happened to our country over the last 50 years, and where are we headed as a result?

What in the world have we been thinking as we teach our younger generation to even want socialism? Did not history teach us this is not the way? Are we not teaching history in our education system? World history clearly reveals the results of what has worked and what has failed? There is evidence that is so obvious today as we view Venezuela and what socialism will produce. Doesn't reality provide a truth that is obvious to everyone?

Our world history is full of socialistic horror stories of how not to govern a nation. Is this reversed thinking from the pit of Eternal damnation as we draw closer to the return of Christ? Why would anyone be moving in this wrong direction while trying to determine the right way?

I keep asking myself, where did we start going wrong? How did I live in America and not see this coming? Was I so into my own life and selfishness that I neglected to pay attention? I'm very saddened to where America is today, and I pray for her immediate return to our God, the Creator of heaven and earth.

I read 1 Chronicles, and pray for His help to raise up His Body of believers and call us all to attention and request His help in this terrible situation unfolding in America today!

> 1 Chronicles 7:14
> *"Then if my people who are called by my name will humble themselves and pray and seek my face and turn from their wicked ways, I will hear from heaven and will forgive their sins and restore their land."*

I'm ashamed that I've sat back and paid no attention to what has been going on and not taken any responsibility to do my part in saving America, the land I love, from where it is headed. Many changes are needed in me, and I need to insert my help and return to our God and pray for America and against the evil forces trying to take her down!

Disaster is written all over this current destructive path we are taking, and we must call upon the Lord to remedy and change this fatal path and protect the nation of America. We must call upon the Lord to come against all evil forces and powers that bring anti-God doctrine into our culture. All practices and ideas that pervert our destiny in the Lord will stagnate the whole reason God raised America up in the first place.

This season of anti-God and false beliefs are strongholds that are contrary to the bible and the God we serve. We are instructed to tear down all strongholds in opposition to the Scriptures and the Truth of God. Our instruction is from the Lord, and we need to heed His directing and turn our nation back over to Him.

But, we must first get ourselves founded in the God of the bible and begin to build a strong foundation on the beliefs given in His Word. Any other thinking that is contrary to Scripture is sinking sand. Then, when storms come, and they certainly will, we must have a solid foundation on which to stand firm. Storms are inevitable, so we must build on His solid ground, or we will be swept away in all the tumultuous activity that storms bring with them.

We are responsible for our choices in life, and we need to be aware of where they will take us and if they will lead us to the Lord. If we don't take responsibility for ourselves, no one else will. Our freedom allows for making choices for ourselves. Our immediate family is directly affected by our decisions, and we must choose carefully. If we choose incorrectly, this leaves us responsible for our bad choices, and there are consequences for each one.

Taking charge of our own lives allows us the opportunity to call upon the Lord. Choosing Him for our salvation and receiving the Holy Spirit is the first thing we must do to build our firm foundation. Once we allow Him to awaken our spirit, we can move forward and start the building process that leads to good spiritual health and godly wisdom.

Listening to the Lord is a necessity, and reading the Word of God will provide His spiritual principles to be used in our learning and growing in the Lord. The scriptural learning gives us a constructive way, and the growth increases our abilities to function better. His Holy Spirit will prompt us and empower us to act out His teachings and make His principles real in our lives.

Learning to block out the worldly clamor that is heard daily is more easily accomplished than you think. It is our choice to whom we listen among all the voices that are coming our direction! Our prayers should include a request to be sensitive to the voice of God!

If what you hear doesn't line up with the Word of God, then it is not His voice speaking to you. Proper identification of the source and what you hear is critical in knowing what voice you are listening. Even your worldly thinking can clutter the voice of God; you need to hear! That's why we need to let Him renew our minds and start to remove any thinking that is in opposition to the Truth of the bible. That's why reading the bible is so very important!

Romans 12:2:
"Don't copy the behavior and customs of this world, but let God transform you into a new person by changing the way you think. Then you will learn to know God's will for you, which is good and pleasing and perfect."

His instructions aren't all that difficult to understand. But, we must be willing, purposely, and prayerful in seeking His wisdom. Our worldly thinking can use a great deal of scriptural understanding and a willingness to follow the Truth rather than the way we are traveling on our own.

Human Reasoning Can Bring False Information

2 Corinthians 10:4:
"We use God's mighty weapons, not worldly weapons, to knock down the strongholds of human reasoning and to destroy false arguments."

A Great Way to Renew our Worldly Thinking

Ephesians 4:23:
"Instead, let the Spirit renew your thoughts and attitudes."

Our mind must be receptive to godly wisdom, or our thinking will not be renewed.

Allow Him to Change You into His Likeness

Colossians 3:10:
"Put on your new nature, and be renewed as you learn to know your Creator and become like him."

Clothe yourself with the righteousness of Christ and smother yourself in His Word. If you don't, you will never renew your knowledge and be changed into His likeness.

Be Strengthened as You Follow Him

> Psalm 23:3:
> *"He renews my strength. He guides me along right paths, bringing honor to his name."*

There is strength in following the Holy Spirit and his guidance made available to us as we learn and allow Him to change us into the likeness of Christ.

His Word Brings Welcomed Change

> Psalm 126:4:
> *"Restore our fortunes, Lord, as streams renew the desert."*

The Lord provides so much to give us an excellent life on earth. Why would anyone choose to refuse His help? Since we have a choice in the matter, what's the problem? Do you think your options are better suited, and that's why you refuse His help?

Do you think you will miss out on the things you want if you develop a relationship with the Lord? Maybe you are under the impression that following Him will cramp your lifestyle or stop you from doing your heart's desire? Did you ever consider His manner of living is a better life than yours?

Whatever you think, please do consider your options and the consequences to follow. Remember there are only two — your's or His. If you serve a God having your best interest at heart and wants you to prosper and be in good health, or is this choice something you don't want? Are you willing to choose your selfish desires at the expense of loosing God's best?

This choosing is something to seriously consider when regarding how you want to live your life. We each want the best life experiences possible — right? So, we each must make a choice and seriously consider all the possibilities. We must understand how important this decision is once all consequences are tallied.

Maybe a list of pros and cons sitting side by side would provide you with a good visual to weigh out what lies ahead. Seeing the consequences for each choice you make today will provide a colorful picture of your future. A clear picture of your future is a great reason as you focus on the results and determine the reality that will manifest in your life.

Should you be a procrastinator, there is even more reason to project your desires on paper and calculate what kind of future you want for yourself. No one else can live your life except you — so, your future is completely in yours hands. And with God's help, it will materialize into a life that is enjoyable, meaningful, prosperous and very rewarding.

Choose Wisely

the

Stage of Life

That you want to entertain

While you're living on earth!

Eternity with God and the
pleasures of this life

will be the results

of your personal decisions.

Conclusion

Every book written has a purpose in mind, or else it won't convey a message the author is trying to make. This book aims to reveal the different stages in life available. The foundation of this message is based using biblical reasoning and wisdom. The idea is to convey what each stage represents and what it provides for each person.

Within each stage, there are variations in numerous areas. These variations can be according to our age, circumstances, seasons, natural and spiritual consequences, and includes many possibilities and combinations. We each select a path in life and posses the freedom to choose which direction we determine to follow.

We each select a path in life and move in that direction. If we realize it does not meet our satisfaction a change may be necessary. We usually learn some paths are better suited for us than others. Should we need to select another direction, our goal is to find the rewards and challenges that are more to our likening.

As people, we collectively make many decisions each day that direct our future. Those choices accumulate and lead us down a specific path in life. The results are directly based on our collective choices. Making good choices will build one upon another

Being aware that any stage in life provides us a limited timeline. During our journey we become more aware that life ends in death for everyone. No one is left out, and the guarantee of physical death is 100%. No one escapes death. Some live longer than others, and this sets the length of time God has allotted. And know this, Scripture tells us no one will live past 120 years maximum (Genesis 6:3).

We come into the world as God directs. There is every indication our entrance has been designated before our birth. God assigns us to our parents, and we have no selection in the process or anything to do with where, when, or what point in time we enter the world.

At conception, we arrive in the womb of the mother God has selected. He carefully knits us together according to the bible — this is Stage 1. Our knitting process take about nine months, then we are physically born into the world. Our physical characteristics are provided by our parents with similarities and differences. Our soul and spirit are contained in this physical body and we become one whole living person — an individual of uniqueness.

At birth, we are helpless and arrive with a *clean slate* with specific DNA, fingerprints, and a mind ready to develop. We must depend on our surroundings (people) and the humans in charge of our care and well-being. Our dependency cannot be avoided, and without proper care and nurturing to increase our development, our outcome will be based on particular set of circumstances and surroundings that we grow and mature within.

Some are advantageous, and some are not. The people in our lives contribute to our living. They provide us with a firsthand experience in life and what is involved in surviving. Sometimes those survival tactics imprison us, and our methods need God's assistance to set us free.

So many different circumstances are available depending where we are born. Our health can be directly affected based on the food and water available to us. Our education, interests, talents, career choices, parental guidance (or lack thereof) provide huge factors. The love and personal care, particular climates, geographic location, culture, economic level, and kinship, all contribute to the person we become in the world as we adapt to the components where we live.

We are born into the world and are automatically given a fallen spiritual status regarding our relationship with God. The Fall of Mankind occurred in the Garden of Eden before we were born, and our personal wrongdoing did not cause this status. It was the sin of disobedience caused by Adam and Eve, and the curse of their sin brought all of humanity into a fallen state.

Many things happen in the world that we have no control over, but remember, we are free to make choices that can help us overcome and conquer the obstacles along the way. It doesn't matter how difficult the path may be; we can choose a way to approach any seemingly impassable barrier from more than one perspective. Most choices are made from feelings, emotions, past experiences, and our reasoning for the logical conclusion.

This kind of perspective is derived from worldly accumulated knowledge only and does not include the Lord. According to the bible, this perspective is viewed from Scripture as typical human choices. The world has much to offer, but if its perspective does not line up with biblical principles found in the bible, our efforts are only temporary and do not touch the root cause of the problem or how best to overcome.

Operating in the physical, using only a worldly perspective limits the realm of available solutions. This human thinking reasons ways to solve issues we each encounter but does not benefit us to the degree that the Lord has made available. And to tap into a best possible solution, we must turn to the Lord for His help, learn to lean on His Word, call on the Holy Spirit, and apply the spiritual principles we find in the bible — our instruction book.

Man has written this book we call the bible as God has instructed the Holy Spirit's power to the spirit of specific individuals. Yes, the different bible chapters reflect the spirit of each writer's personality, but their prompting came as the Holy Spirit directed each of them (2 Timothy 3:16; 2 Peter 1:20, 21).

Now — that is where the resistance begins to emerge from our spirit man because the spiritual realm is not a natural approach, because it is not in line with our natural thinking. How do we emerge from this natural state of worldly thinking? We must be open to the spiritual world where we live and begin to understand what we're up against and how we must operate to get the best results.

We usually come to the end of ourselves as we try to resolve every problem alone. And many times, we exhaust ourselves before giving in and asking for help from someone else. This single-handed approach becomes a pressure point that hopefully causes us to be open to outside help — God's!

From the world's perspective it appears that support is all around us, but it may not be sufficient to overcome and solve our problems. This kind of help can be of benefit but does not always deal with the real issue or remove the cause of the problem. Without removing the root cause, the problem remains and symptoms reoccur. Our relief in the future is directly dependent on the removal of the root cause!

The extent of our physical existence does depend on the spiritual as well. We don't just live in a physical world. The world in which we live has an unseen spiritual realm. This spiritual realm very definitely has direct affects on our living life and has specific characteristics that cause difficulties in living. These issues must be resolved to live life to the fullest.

The bible tells us of its existence, and that it must be dealt with, and that we are not capable of operating in the flesh to resist its negative impact. The Lord works through the Holy Spirit and that too operates through the spiritual realm. And, we need to receive spiritual guidance from the Lord in order to overcome.

So, what are we to do? We are to learn about this spiritual realm and understand how it operates in the world we live in, and determine what is required to guard against any spiritual warfare. We are to learn how to fully function in this spiritual realm, and use the bible for instructions to operate with understanding of how it operate.

The Lord utilized the spiritual realm to operate through the Holy Spirit. Satan has a counterfeit and he operates bringing warfare against us and squelch the voice of God. We discussed earlier about identifying which voice your listening to and its origin.

We must refer to the Bible to help us understand how to defend ourselves against any harmful effects it may bring and learn how to stay protected from the bad and in touch with the good.

We are born into the world and are subject to influence and attacks that exist and functions in Satan's spiritual realm. When we receive the Lord we open up the spiritual realm that the Lord functions through — the Holy Spirit! Our help flows through God's Spirit and we must learn to operate by following the voice of God. Our learning and growing in the Spirit of God will only find confirmation through this awareness of Him.

Learning to listen to the Lord will be in direct conflict with Satan's spiritual guidance and we must learn the difference. Satan has been allowed his counterfeit to God's Spirit so we have a choice in our future and to whom we want to listen to. We refer to the bible to help understand how to guard ourselves from any harmful effects Satan brings and learn how to stay protected from its evil while staying in touch with the Lord.

Review with me several biblical references that deal with the many questions that come to the surface when the subject of spiritual reality is discussed. I have listed below several Scriptures that I pray will increase your understanding and cause you to find the answers needed to comprehend more about this unseen reality — So, let the Scriptures speak for themselves:

God Formed the Earth from The Spirit

> Genesis 1:2:
> *"The earth was formless and empty, and darkness covered the deep waters. And the **Spirit** of God was hovering over the surface of the waters."*

> Leviticus 20:6:
> *"I will also turn against those who commit **spirit**ual prostitution by putting their trust in mediums or in those who consult the **spirit**s of the dead. I will cut them off from the community."*

God can Make Certain our Victory

Judges 3:10:
*"The **Spirit** of the Lord came upon him, and he became Israel's judge. He went to war against King Cushan-rishathaim of Aram, and the Lord gave Othniel victory over him."*

The Lord Brings Strength beyond Human Ability

Judges 14:6:
"At that moment the Spirit of the Lord came powerfully upon him, and he ripped the lion's jaws apart with his bare hands. He did it as easily as if it were a young goat. But he didn't tell his father or mother about it."

God Uses Man to Speak for Him

1 Samuel 10:6:
"At that time the Spirit of the Lord will come powerfully upon you, and you will prophesy with them. You will be changed into a different person."

God's Holy Spirit Lead the Israelites as they Crossed the Desert

Nehemiah 9:20:
"You sent your good Spirit to instruct them, and you did not stop giving them manna from heaven or water for their thirst."

God can Direct our Hearts Desire if we but Ask

Psalm 51:10:
"Create in me a clean heart, O God. Renew a loyal spirit within me."

The Spirit of God Teaches us Foundational Truths

Psalm 143:10:
*"Teach me to do your will, for you are my God. May your gracious **Spirit** lead me forward on a firm footing."*

God is Able to See our Every Motive

Proverbs 20:27:
*"The Lord's light penetrates the human **spirit**, exposing every hidden motive."*

The Spirit of God Divides the Fleshly from the Spiritual

Jeremiah 9:25:
"A time is coming," says the Lord, "when I will punish all those who are circumcised in body but not in spirit —"

A City Living in Spiritual Darkness without God's Spirit

Jonah 4:11:
"But Nineveh has more than 120,000 people living in spiritual darkness, not to mention all the animals. Shouldn't I feel sorry for such a great city?"

God's Holy Spirit Gives Mankind the Ability to Cast out Evil Spirits

Matthew 10:1:
"Jesus called his twelve disciples together and gave them authority to cast out evil spirits and to heal every kind of disease and illness."

Matthew 12:43:
"When an evil spirit leaves a person, it goes into the desert, seeking rest but finding none."

The Evil Spirits Knew Jesus

Mark 3:11:
"And whenever those possessed by evil spirits caught sight of him, the spirits would throw them to the ground in front of him shrieking, 'You are the Son of God!'"

Where Does Spiritual Life Begin? Only Through Accepting Jesus

John 3:6:
"Humans can reproduce only human life, but the Holy Spirit gives birth to spiritual life."

The Mystery of being Born Again

John 3:8:
"The wind blows wherever it wants. Just as you can hear the wind but can't tell where it comes from or where it is going, so you can't explain how people are born of the Spirit."

John 7:39:
"When he said, 'living water,' he was speaking of the Spirit, who would be given to everyone believing in him. But the Spirit had not yet been given, because Jesus had not yet entered into his glory."

What is Spiritual Blindness?

John 9:35-40:
When Jesus heard what had happened, he found the man and asked, "Do you believe in the Son of Man?" The man answered, "Who is he, sir? I want to believe in him."

"You have seen him," Jesus said, "and he is speaking to you!" "Yes, Lord, I believe!" the man said. And he worshiped Jesus."

"Then Jesus told him, 'I entered this world to render judgment—to give sight to the blind and to show those who think they see that they are blind,'" (2 Corinthians 3:16).

"Some Pharisees who were standing nearby heard him and asked, 'Are you saying we're blind?'"

Jesus was revealing to the religious establishment that our physical visibility does not see the things of God. Spiritual blindness is all we can experience without Christ in our lives.

So then, Who is Blind?

2 Corinthians 4:4:
"Satan, who is the god of this world, has blinded the minds of those who don't believe. They are unable to see the glorious light of the Good News. They don't understand this message about the glory of Christ, who is the exact likeness of God."

The Holy Spirit is our Guide to Finding God's Truth

John 16:13:
"When the Spirit of truth comes, he will guide you into all truth. He will not speak on his own but will tell you what he has heard. He will tell you about the future."

And who Does the Holy Spirit hear From? The Heart of God!

Romans 2:29:
"No, a true Jew is one whose heart is right with God. And true circumcision is not merely obeying the letter

of the law; rather, it is a change of heart produced by the Spirit. And a person with a changed heart seeks praise from God, not from people."

How do You Receive your Spiritual Sight?

2 Thessalonians 3:3:
"But the Lord is faithful; he will strengthen you and guard you from the evil one. And we are confident in the Lord that you are doing and will continue to do the things we commanded you. May the Lord lead your hearts into a full understanding and expression of the love of God and the patient endurance that comes from (knowing) Christ."

This living by faith is God's new way for us to live abundantly. We are to accept Christ and receive our Salvation through faith in Him (Romans 3:22). Receiving our Salvation and living in obedience to His Word gives us His spiritual eyesight and enlightenment through His wisdom and principles in application!

Our spiritual vision is from the Lord and gives us eyes to see and ears to hear His voice and receive His understanding that, before receiving Christ in our lives, was not possible. As previously said — our physical vision does not see the things of God.

Galatians 3:22:
"But the Scriptures declare that we are all prisoners of sin, so we receive God's promise of freedom only by believing in Jesus Christ."

Romans 7:6:
"But now we have been released from the law, for we died to it and are no longer captive to its power. Now we can serve God, not in the old way of obeying the letter of the law, but in the new way of living in the Spirit."

Romans 8:4:

"He did this so that the just requirement of the law would be fully satisfied for us, who no longer follow our sinful nature but instead follow the Spirit."

It Really Matters Who is Leading Us

Romans 8:6:

"So letting your sinful nature control your mind leads to death. But letting the Spirit control your mind leads to life and peace."

The Spirit of God will Take You Home at Life's End

Romans 8:10:

"And Christ lives within you, so even though your body will die because of sin, the Spirit gives you life because you have been made right with God."

Our Hope for Eternity

Romans 8:23:

"And we believers also groan, even though we have the Holy Spirit within us as a foretaste of future glory, for we long for our bodies to be released from sin and suffering. We, too, wait with eager hope for the day when God will give us our full rights as his adopted children, including the new bodies he has promised us."

Romans 8:26:

"And the Holy Spirit helps us in our weakness. For example, we don't know what God wants us to pray for. But the Holy Spirit prays for us with groanings that cannot be expressed in words."

Romans 8:27:

"And the Father who knows all hearts knows what the Spirit is saying, for the Spirit pleads for us believers in harmony with God's own will."

Romans 15:13:

"I pray that God, the source of hope, will fill you completely with joy and peace because you trust in him. Then you will overflow with confident hope through the power of the Holy Spirit."

It is so exciting to learn that there is more to living than what we see with the natural eye. Life without the Lord is limited because our physical abilities cannot deal with the spiritual world in which we live. Because we cannot see it with our natural vision, what is all around us is not seen or a means to determine it does or does not exist.

Learning through Scripture how to deal with the forces of evil through the saving grace of Christ opens up a future that includes His empowerment to handle the world around us with greater ease and sufficient power to be effective in defeating the enemy.

Learning and receiving His help and applying His principles to our everyday living takes us into Stage 5 and utilizes more of what His death on the Cross provides. God has a plan, and the Lord sent His Son, Jesus, to give us help in living out our lives on earth. We weren't just dropped in at birth and left to fend for ourselves. Jesus has provided a way!

As we progress further along in the Stages of Life, we come to Stage 6. This stage is new to me because I didn't even know it existed. I have been in church my whole life and never even heard about seeking the Lord to this extent. It is a place of rest and peace that surpasses anything I could imagine or had hoped. It is a place of peace that passes my understanding but is very welcomed and enjoyable.

When I first started to write this book, I told the Lord I had no idea what Stage 6 entailed, and He would have to let me know what I was to learn as I listened to His voice. In short order, He led me to a teaching that touched on the idea but was vague, and I still didn't realize the fullness of this stage.

As I pursued the Lord, I started to learn about this spiritual awareness of coming closer to the Lord as I prayed and worshipped Him. It was a surprise to my understanding because I didn't know what was going to take place. I don't intend for this to sound too far out there, but I believe the Lord wants all of us to seek Him above all else and yield our lives to Him fully and submit our will to develop a deeper relationship with Him.

I believe He wants each of us to follow after Him as closely as we can, be open to His closeness, not to block out where it might take us, and resist because it is unknown. I don't think our learning ever ends, and the Lord wants peace on earth in our heart, mind, and spirit before He takes us home to spend eternity with Him.

To pursue a closer relationship with the Lord is an opportunity to know Him better, sense the condition of His heart, and see more of what He is like that cannot be understood any other way. Our God desires fellowship with us while living on earth and wants to express Himself through us while we're living here. Why? Because that is the way He wants to befriend us, and help us grow in relationship with Him, as well as, complete His plan and use us to accomplish His purpose.

Throughout the bible, I see that God has continued to reveal Himself in many different ways and to many different people. I believe He is still doing just that, and since we are living in the latter days that His presence is ever extending, which allows us to be closer to Him than any generation before us.

When He returns, there will be signs of His coming happening on the earth and our generation today is seeing many of the signs talked about in the bible (Matthew, chapter 24). Scripture tells us to be prepared, and growing in relationship with Him will accomplish just that. We don't want to become so distracted with events and circumstances that we neglect the Lord, who not only created us but wants to take us home.

Then, we will experience an eternal relationship that will continue to grow and flourish and give us everything we could ever dream of in a never-ending time frame that only exists for those who have answered His call and received His Salvation.

Stage 7

Won't you answer His calling and accept His Salvation offer by faith in Christ and begin your journey to peace on earth and everlasting life with Him?

Romans 3:30:
"There is only one God, and he makes people right with himself only by faith, whether they are Jews or Gentiles."

About the Author

Doug Poole spent his life between 0-12 growing up on a farm in Oklahoma and then moving to Wichita, Kansas until eighteen. Completing high school at Wichita South, then on to college at the University of Oklahoma. The Marine Corps, Okinawa, and Vietnam occupied his time until getting married in 1971.

His 42 years of marriage (1st wife deceased) caused him to turn from his single thinking and become involved with a family. The family he got was exactly what he had asked the Lord for and came as a package ready to be enjoyed.

Years of training was necessary to teach him that God's ways were quite different from his and that he needed more training than he first thought.

His life on the farm growing up, and his godly grandparents proved to be foundational in his development for what was coming in the future.

With the school of hard knocks and the Lord woven all through his life, it brought him in his seventies to finally arrive where God wanted him the whole time.

Now remarried, a season of remembrance and biblical principles have finally persuaded him to seek the Lord for a new adventure. And, that new adventure has been to share with others what God has taught him and to reference God's principles in the writing of several books.

www.DougPoole.net

Other books by author

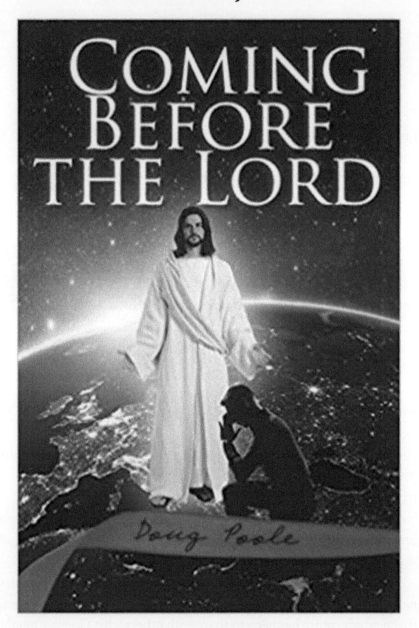

Coming Before the LORD
December 3, 2019
by Doug Poole (Author)

Can we have a personal relationship with God today?

What does it require to become a believer?

Is it possible to enter the presence of God like they did in the OT?

Can anything from an old book like the Bible be used today?

Does applying the Scriptures in the twenty-first century really answer today's questions for living life to the fullest?

The Old and New Testaments reveal much about the character of God. Examples of both good and evil are revealed for our learning. The results of both good and evil are explained in detail, and we can see the results of each choice. As we read through the bible, we see evidence of God's plan for mankind and opportunities to become more acquainted with Him.

Working together with the Holy Spirit provides guidance and understanding that are intended to strengthen and help us. This wisdom has practical applications that provide a better way to handle life. He has revealed ways we can use to personalize a relationship with Him that can grow over time.

Entering His Presence is possible today because of what Christ accomplished by his death, burial, and resurrection. The finished work of Christ has opened a gateway to the throne of God that was not available to each believer before. We become like the priests of old and have access to the Father.

Old Testament rituals have been replaced with New Testament opportunities that seek Him and receive help and understanding. The sending of the Holy Spirit has provided us with the Helper that resides inside of every believer. We can have a personal relationship with our Creator.

Entering His Presence is possible today because Christ broke down the barrier that once stood between God and man.

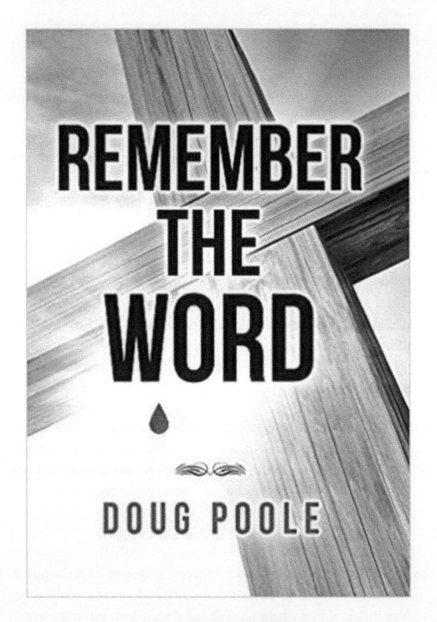

Remember the WORD
February 25, 2020
by Doug Poole (Author)

This book provides stories and testimonials of experiences discovered from the Word of God in my personal life. It brings lives of biblical characters into real-time applications and the challenges they encountered.

Practical solutions are provided to the reader and appear throughout the book with reflection on both failures and triumphs woven into the many categories it covers. Experiencing the Lord is as common today as it was in biblical times. Our culture is quite different but principles and applications of God's Word still apply today.

Don't judge a book by its cover has been a rule taught to many generations. Its origin is ancient but the same applies in the modem world in which we live. Looking at the cover of a bible may look ancient but its contents and principles will amaze you. Get under the old cover you see on the outside and get into its contents and discoverer its wisdom for yourself on the inside.

The Diagram

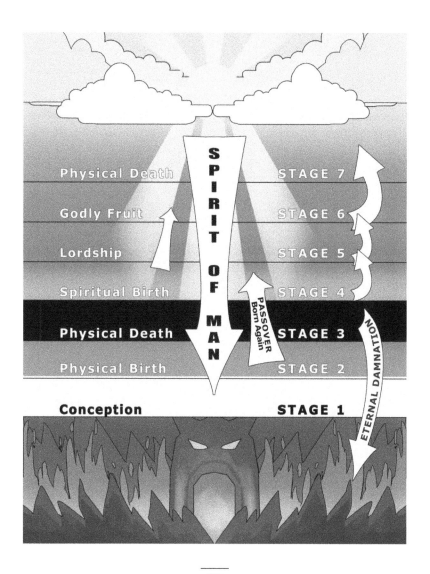

APPENDIX II

My Concept — The Trinity by Doug Poole

To explain the Trinity is not a simple task. Doing so is similar to providing a brilliant mathematician with a formula that works very well to resolve a specific problem area but does not encompass the entire solution. It satisfies with repetitive accuracy a segment but still leaves a great deal unresolved to the whole situation and surrounding circumstances.

He can see the concept in fundamental principles, but he knows there is still a great deal unresolved to his knowledge and understanding. He can see the idea in basic principles, but he knows there is a much broader concept unexplained than the formula provides. Because of this, more knowledge is warranted to resolve and understand completely.

There are many diagrams of the Christian Trinity, and most seem to give us a mental picture of what is explained from Scripture. Still, there seems to be more needed to grasp the massive nature and all God represents. Somehow, we don't seem to be able to explain all the possibilities that may exist in an illustration.

I have looked at numerous diagrams on the internet but decided to present what I believe is a diagram of the Trinity. My attempt is according to my understanding, and conception as I read through the bible. Obviously, I have not reached a conclusive diagram that captures the entirety of God. My finite attempt is too simple to capture His fullness. I don't think humanity understands enough about God to reach an exact pictorial illustration.

The following illustrated concept captures the Father, Son, and Holy Spirit which are three separate persons exhibiting portions of God's character. Each have a definite function in presenting the concepts of Scripture but not the entirety of God.

Each person making up the Trinity is a separate and real expression of God. They are instrumental in providing function, express God's wisdom, exhibiting God's character, and provide help to humankind. God does His work on the earth today utilizing people to fulfill His very purpose. So, here is what I see in the bible about our God using my visual concept to contemplate a possible concept of Him.

The Trinity provides all we need to be used and changed to the likeness of Christ and become the purpose of God for mankind. Each member of the Trinity reflects a portion of God for humanity to experience and utilize. The offering of Himself is necessary for each believer to overcome the environment in which we exist and to flourish as God intends.

He provides us with all the wisdom, strength, power and armor to combat the evil spiritual world where we exist. He is totally aware of our conditions, and He knows we will prosper using His provisions, and become His hands and feet functioning on the earth.

He knows our every weaknesses because He's been here [the Son] and understands we require His help to be overcomers. He provides all we need to be victorious. That is, if we will but choose to follow His biblical principles [the Word], accept Salvation from His Son [Jesus Christ], put our actions in obedience to His guidelines [biblical principles], and follow the promptings from His Holy Spirit.

The fullness of God is yet to be captured as we attempt to visualize His spiritual being in a simple diagram compiled and provided by finite understanding. God's essence and fullness far exceed our knowledge or abilities to capture Him with understanding and certainly not on paper in a colorful diagram.

He is God, and that giving of Himself to humanity is our opportunity to receive His offerings that will lead us back home to spend eternity with Him!

Lightning Source UK Ltd.
Milton Keynes UK
UKHW012150270521
384511UK00007B/652/J